J. C. PENNEY, MERCHANT PRINCE

J. C. Penney, Merchant Prince

A Biography of a Man Who Built a
Business Empire Based on the Golden Rule

by

BEATRICE PLUMB

Publishers

T. S. DENISON & COMPANY, INC.

Minneapolis

Other Books in the Men of Achievement Series

This book is prayerfully dedicated
to all
who obey the golden rule,
or sincerely try to.

Foreword

Of the many books that have been written by or about or in collaboration with J. C. Penney, this volume is, in my opinion, the very best. The author has sensitivity, a penetrating understanding of the life whose history she tells, and on these pages she makes the man himself come alive.

It has been my good fortune to be intimately associated with Mr. Penney for nearly forty years. Through these decades, during which he reached the guarded heights of character and achievement which made him pre-eminent among all merchants in America, and during which he also suffered reverses that practically wiped out his fortune and brought him physically close to death, I have found in him those qualities that mark him as a rock, as a strong tower, as a truly good and great man. My figures are mixed even as my emotions are mixed when I think of my friend.

Chiefly it is as a friend that I think of him. Even in his business relationships, friendship has marked him. Long ago he was named the "man with a thousand partners." Well, that "thousand" has now become "thousands." But neither by addition, multiplication or possible subtraction does the number ever affect the quality of his relationship with those in whom he has placed his confidence. When such an associate has failed, I have watched him as he has taken on part of the man's failure and made it as his own.

I have known him to relocate men once, even twice, and perhaps yet again. Again and again, his faith and his acute understanding of human personality has been rewarded. Failure in one city, or even a second, has become a success in yet another. This quality in J. C. Penney often amazed and always thrilled me.

As Beatrice Plumb retells the story, when he found God, after his all but fatal physical ordeal, he found the yet more abundant life, and he lives now in his high eighties with a triumphant voice that makes his soul articulate in time and space and out beyond!

Our second son, Clark, the youngest of the Four Chaplains of the Three Faiths, who went down on the S.S. Dorchester when this troopship was sunk by torpedoes in the North Atlantic during World War II, loved and revered Mr. Penney. Theirs was a unique friendship. Following a football season at Oakwood School in Poughkeepsie, New York, Clark came down with double pneumonia. For a time, he was seriously ill. Early in his convalescence, Mr. Penney came to me and said, "Dan, let me have Clark in Florida. Let me give him the sunshine and care that he needs." And so Clark went to be with Mr. Penney and Penney's youngest son, Kimball, who was then a little boy. Those four months that our son spent with the great merchant marked him for life. So long as he lived, he was not only grateful to this mature friend but he loved Mr. Penney with the purpose to build a life like his. A few months ago, Mr. Penney gave me two letters Clark had written him after that Florida experience, and now our grandson, Clark Jr., and our granddaughter, Susan, who was born after the Dorchester went down, will have them.

This, then, is the man whose story is told on these pages. A story that will be an inspiration, I know— an inspiration and a challenge to a multitude of boys and girls, young men and young women of this and yet other generations.   —Daniel A. Poling

Preface

I first met Mr. Penney in 1930. I had driven hundreds of miles to Green Cove Springs, Florida, where I asked an attendant at the Springs if he could direct me to the Qui-Si-Sana Hotel, where I was to meet Mr. Penney for an interview.

"Just across the road," directed the attendant. "It belongs to J. C. Penney. Ever met him? A grand fellow; straight as they come."

Of that first meeting, I wrote, "Five minutes later, I saw him coming towards me in the hotel. I had seen that face pictured many times before, always with a certain indomitable expression there, a forcefulness back of a quite alarming aloofness.

"But about this man who came towards me with outstretched hand was something that had eluded the camera. An entirely likable something. What struck me first was his simplicity of appearance, dress and manner; the absence of any air of importance. Nothing to suggest the business magnate, the captain of industry. Instead I instantly remembered that he was the son of a small-town minister.

"A straightforward man with the clear eyes of a clear thinker, direct and true. He walked with a straight, firm tread. He spoke deliberately, with no waste of words, right to the point. Yes, I decided, if I had to describe him in a single word, it would be 'straight.' Then he looked directly at me, and smiled, and suddenly I knew why he was 'Golden Rule Penney.' It was that sort of a smile."

Thirty years passed before I interviewed him again. This was at Camelback Inn, Phoenix, Arizona, where he was enjoying a short vacation with his grandchildren. To me, he looked exactly the same, "straight as they come," and with the same Golden Rule smile.

And again, in the same year, I met him in the Florida home of his nephew, a retired Penney manager. The previous day Mr. Penney had attended the elaborate opening ceremony of a new Penney store in Fort Lauderdale, the largest suburban one in the chain, with its 100,000 square feet of shining, blue and white efficiency.

It was a gala day. He was being honored at luncheons and dinners. There were radio and press appointments he must meet. Luggage stood in the hall, a car at the door ready to start for the airport. Would he have a minute to spare for me?

He came to the door to welcome me, and again he looked exactly the same, "straight as they come," and with the same Golden Rule smile. Founder of a business that the previous year had grossed one billion, 500 million dollars, this son of a small-town minister again found time to grant me another unhurried interview.

My thanks go first to him. Next to his executive secretary, Mrs. Eva McLaughlin, for her friendly, patient help. Then to the books written by Mr. Penney, or about him:

MAIN STREET MERCHANT by Norman Beasley; J. C. PENNEY, THE MAN WITH A THOUSAND PARTNERS, as told to Robert W. Buere; FIFTY YEARS WITH THE GOLDEN RULE by J. C. Penney, in collaboration with Miss Janet Mabie; MR. PENNEY by Harry J. Albus; VIEW FROM THE NINTH DEC-

ADE by J. C. Penney; LINES OF A LAYMAN by J. C. Penney.

My thanks go also to the writers of numerous articles about Mr. Penney, which have appeared in magazines from 1920 to the present year. And a special thank you to Samuel Feinberg for a series of articles he wrote about Mr. Penney under the title, "From where I sit," in "Women's Wear Daily."

The Author

Contents

Chapter One

Basic Training for a Business Career

In a little white house, under a stand of maple trees in the little farming town of Hamilton, Missouri, a curly-haired, eight-year-old boy named Jim Penney, tossed unhappily in his bed, trying to grapple with a big problem—holes in his shoes!

Until the previous evening, the problem would have been his father's. But no longer. Now it was up to him to earn the money to buy all his own clothes.

It was not unusual in that part of rural Missouri, in the year 1884, for boys as young as he to start to earn. Jim's older brother on the farm had been earning his own money for years, raising chickens, sheep, crops, helping neighborhood farmers, even doing an occasional job in town. But how could a little boy, "going on nine," earn anything?

Yet his father had said, "You can do it, Jim. Just try. You'll find a way." And his mother had smiled, "That's for you to figure out, son. You'll think of something."

For hours he had been thinking. He tossed and thought . . . tossed and thought. In an attempt to figure out something, he went over in his mind the surprising events of the previous evening. He had been doing his homework, as usual, when his father had called him to come into his study. His father was sitting at his desk, working on his Sunday sermon. Nothing unusual about that. Then had come the shock!

"Jim," he had said, "your mother and I have talked it over, and have decided that you are now old enough to buy your own clothes."

Could he be joking? No. His father joked about some things, but never about so serious a thing as money. He meant it!

Jim had sat in that big study chair for several stunned seconds before saying, "Yes, sir," from force of habit. Then he had wriggled his toes, and remembered his shoes, with a hole in each sole.

"Pa, won't you buy me one more pair?"

"No, Jim. You will have to begin now to earn all those things for yourself."

Little Jim's head twisted on the pillow, his mind, for the first time in his eight years of carefree living, suddenly confronted with the immediate need to earn money. Could he run errands, he wondered, two cents for a short one, five cents for a long one? Could he collect rags and bones for the junk man? But that would bring him only a few pennies. He needed at least a dollar for a new pair of shoes—and, even at that, they would be the very cheap sort the other boys would tease him about when he wore them.

Finally, his gray eyes, wet with tears, misted over, and the worried little boy who one day would be the founder of the largest retail department store chain in the world, whose name would be over more than seventeen hundred stores in America, slept, his dreams an uneasy mixture of a jay's nest with four eggs in it, and his two shoes, with a big hole in each sole.

Little Jim did not know that his father, for whom he was named, had definite ideas about teaching his children the value of money, and the right way to earn it.

His father, James Cash Penney, a minister's son, was born in Missouri. He went to Kentucky as a young man, and after marrying his beloved Mary Frances, he stayed on there for some time to teach school, preach and farm. Then came the Civil War, and he returned to Missouri to enlist. At the end of the war, young James Cash Penney, then twenty-four, pioneered to Missouri to establish a farm home on raw land near Hamilton.

Although a hard-working man, he was not a money-maker. There was a heavy mortgage on his farm of almost 400 acres of pasture land, and another on the home he had bought in Hamilton so that his children could be near schools. There was little cash money, always debts, and, for all his faith in the providence of God, a lurking fear of privation for his family. It was of utmost importance to him that he should teach his children self-reliance.

"If I had ten boys and a million dollars," he was wont to say in his quiet, convincing way, "I wouldn't give them a dime." He saw to it that each of his own was given an early chance to learn what was needed to make an honest living.

Little Jim, not yet nine, set out to learn to be self-reliant. He covered his school slate with hopeful figures. Meanwhile, the holes in his shoes grew bigger, and his father and mother, and his older brother and sister continued to tell him when he begged them to give him some idea of how he could earn the price of a pair of shoes, "You'll think of something. We had to."

Then one day he got his chance! Elie, Jim's older brother, had a conflict in jobs. He had promised his father to bring in the hay that day, forgetting that he had already promised a neighboring farmer to work for him. How could he be in two places at once?

Little Jim's heart gave a sudden jump. Was this an "earning" job? It was a good question, for many of the home and farm chores were done by the boys as their fair share of the work load, and no pay expected.

"Does Pa pay you for bringing in the hay?" Jim wanted to know.

Elie ruefully assured him that their father did. As much as twenty-five cents a load, and there would probably be from six to eight loads.

Jim was getting better at arithmetic. Having to earn his clothes made figuring good sense, not just school stuff.

His heart beating faster, he asked, "Could I bring in that hay? If I did, would Pa pay me, the same as you?"

Elie saw it as a possible way out of his predicament. "Ask him," he suggested.

Jim catapulted into the barn where his father was working. Breathlessly, he told of Elie's plight, and his own willingness to take his place—and his pay.

His father gave him one of his rare smiles. It was a deal, as one farmer to another. "And if you do a good job, you can bring the hay in from the other field tomorrow."

"New shoes!" exulted little Jim.

"Don't forget you have more than shoes to buy," warned his father.

For two days, the boy worked in the hayfield, proudly bringing in load after load to the barn. Until there were fourteen loads there—and three dollars and fifty cents in his hand. One dollar went for shoes —the first he had ever bought with his own money.

"They were cheap shoes, even for those times," remembers J. C. Penney, "brogans of cowhide, black and clumsy, put together with wooden pegs, fastened over the instep with coarse enameled buckles, like those on overshoes. I was disappointed in them, but they were the best I could afford. I felt a little comforted after I took off the ugly buckles and used just the eyelets."

He had two dollars and fifty cents left. He could spend it at once for another shirt and cotton stockings, or—and here the business man began to sprout— he could invest it in something that brought him a profit with which he could buy the clothes he needed. But what could he invest in?

"That's for you to figure out, son," his mother had said. "You'll think of something." And, all of a sudden he did! PIGS! Didn't his father make money fattening stock in his pasture? Then why couldn't a little boy buy a little pig and fatten it?

Late that afternoon, Farmer Jones, milking his cows on a nearby farm, was surprised to see Preacher Penney's little lad at his elbow.

"How much would one of your little pigs cost me?" he wanted to know, with a bargaining glint in his eye.

Farmer Jones blinked. What on earth did the child want a pig for? To fatten and sell, Jim explained, so that he could buy himself some new clothes.

Farmer Jones nodded, fully understanding. He said he was getting between three and four dollars for one, but since Jim had only two dollars and fifty cents, he would let him have a small pig for this amount.

Joyfully, Jim carried the squealing piglet home in his arms. He put it in a box in the barn, gave it what he could find to eat and drink, then strode manfully in to supper. But his problems were not over, for now he must find a way to get food for his pig. He had no money left with which to buy it. He noticed that his pig spurned the nice new grass he gave it, but gobbled down the stale old apple and potato peelings thrown out from the farm kitchen.

That gave him an idea. Other people had such leftovers. They called them swill. Why not collect these from the nearby neighbors? In return, he could offer to wash out the containers, returning the empties clean and sweet-smelling.

The idea worked. Neighbors gratefully accepted

such service, glad to have their kitchen garbage carried away, and everything left shipshape.

Jim was now in business! He built a pen for his pig, and a wooden feeding trough. Soon he was following the farm corn huskers, gathering up the waste ears, so that he had enough corn to feed his pig all winter.

He was growing up. He had tried hard, and found a way. He had proved he could do it—just as his father had said!

Chapter Two

Jim Learns the Golden Rule

Jim was ten years old, and once more he tossed unhappily in his bed, this time trying to grapple with something that was destined to be the biggest thing in his life—the Golden Rule, as applied to everyday living, even his job.

What had the Golden Rule to do with his pigs? As he saw it, in his affronted, small boy way, nothing. Yet his father had said, siding with the complaining neighbors, "Do unto others as you would be done by." Jim knew that his father was thinking of something Jesus had said, away off in Bible days—"Therefore all things whatsoever ye would that men should do to you, do ye even so to them." For Jim was familiar with the Scriptures. He went to Sunday school twice each Sunday—to the Baptist in the morning, to the Presbyterian in the afternoon.

But that "unto others" was Sunday talk. This was a weekday. What had that text to do with his pigs?

Ten-year-old Jim had not yet learned that there

was no separation between his father's Sunday and weekday religion; that he always practiced what he preached, and served God as wholeheartedly in the pig pen as he did in the pulpit.

Jim was hurt, and baffled, and angry. His pig business had been going so well. The first one had thrived, and he had sold it to buy more pigs. Now he had a dozen, well on their way to becoming pork. He had sensed his father's quiet approval of the way he was learning to be self-reliant, and able to buy his own clothes.

He was fattening his pigs for the market. They were not yet heavy enough, but in the next four or five months they would be. Then he could sell them, buy more, and still have money left to buy new clothes for himself, and—maybe—even have a little bit left over to put in the bank.

That dreadful night, two years ago, when his father had told him that from now on he must buy all his own clothes, he had cried as he tossed. Now he was too big for tears! Yet the order his father had now given was just as shocking—to sell his pigs at once, get what he could for them in their half-fattened condition, and then stop raising them.

Why? Because the neighbors objected to their smell and noise!

What right, fumed Jim, had the neighbors to complain? Didn't the pigs belong to him? What business were his pigs to the neighbors? And wasn't he doing those same neighbors a good turn by collecting their swill, and cleaning out their smelly old pails? Besides, no matter how one tried to keep a pig sty clean, it smelled bad. Didn't his father want him to earn money?

Jim decided he would ask his father that, first thing in the morning, and make one more plea to be allowed to keep his pigs just five more months, when he could get top price for them.

Next morning, he grabbed his first chance to ask that pointed question. "Pa, don't you want me to make money?"

"Yes; but not at other people's expense."

"What does that mean?"

"That you have no right to make money if by so doing you are taking advantage of other people. When you had one or two pigs, there was no complaint from the neighbors. Now that you have so many, they complain of the smell and the noise. And I can't rightly blame them. If we lived miles away from the next farm, that would be another matter. But we have close neighbors, and you, as well as I, must protect their rights. You must sell your pigs."

"How soon, Pa?"

"Tomorrow, without fail."

Jim searched his father's stern face for any sign of reprieve. There was none. Nor was there any trace of compromise from his mother. "You must be a good neighbor, son," she said, and smiled at him.

With a heavy heart, he sold his pigs, receiving only half of what he had counted on. Still, they brought him sixty dollars, more money than he had ever possessed in his life.

There were two banks in the little town of Hamilton, and now Jim took a hard look at both. He knew that banks sometimes failed. Which one looked the least likely to, with his wealth in it? At last he decided to put thirty dollars in the first, and thirty dollars in the second. Then, he reasoned, if one failed, he would still have enough left in the other to buy shoes and clothes.

He hurried home with his two bank books to show his father, and was happy to see his approving smile, and hear him tell his mother, "I believe Jim is going to make a good business man."

But his happiness was short-lived as his father added, "Now you'll have to figure out another way to earn money."

It was hard to do. He could not make much running errands for nearby neighbors, with an occasional pay-job from his father. He was soon drawing on his money in the two banks, and fast growing out of his clothes.

In the lean years that followed, Jim searched everywhere for means of making money. "You'll find a way," his father encouraged him. "Keep on trying."

Then came the news of a horse auction downtown. Jim took new heart. Why couldn't he buy a young colt, raise it, and sell it at a profit? His father, having lived in Kentucky, knew a great deal about horses. Would he go with him and help him select a good one?

"No," said his father, positively. "You must learn to make your own decisions, Jim. That's all a part of learning how to make money. If you are going to be a horse-trader, you must learn how by your own experience, not mine."

"But you know more about horses than I do."

"Yes; but it is up to you to learn all the tricks of the trade yourself. You'll have to find out for yourself if there's anything wrong with the horse you are looking at. Don't expect others to tell you, least of all the man who wants to trade or sell it. Just keep your eyes open, that's all."

"But, Pa, what if I make a mistake?"

"Then you will have learned something. That's experience—first-hand experience. Nothing like it!"

Jim talked long and earnestly with his father about the tricky game of trading or selling horses, "a game of pretty strict rules." Then he set forth, resolved that nobody should put anything over on him. He would not be an easy one to cheat.

He examined every horse, alertly on guard. He listened to the horsy talk preceding other deals. Then he selected a mare, a handsome colt that anyone would be proud to own. He led her home, thrilled that he had been able to buy so fine looking an animal with his own money. He patted her with an owner's affection as he put her in the barn and went in to supper.

He had so much to tell about the horse fair, but he had barely started before he was interrupted by a terrific racket coming from the barn. Thuds, crashes, the splintering of wood! Was something happening to his horse? He dashed out to the barn, his father at his heels.

Something was happening to the barn, not the horse! The new colt had already kicked out one side of her stall, and was rapidly demolishing the other.

Jim's eyes widened in dismay. Had he made a bad choice? But perhaps it was the strange barn that scared her. By tomorrow she might have quieted down.

But tomorrow she was still kicking everything she could reach into smithereens. And the next day, and the next. Then Jim realized that this handsome colt was a wild one, a bad actor, with a mean streak in her that he could do nothing about.

"Looks like I made a bad mistake, Pa," he lamented. It did not comfort him at all when his father pointed out that this experience had taught him a valuable lesson—not to judge things by their outward appearance; to try to become a more careful, shrewd buyer.

Jim had to sell his beautiful little animal for less than he paid for her. That was a hard blow. "Instead of making money, I lost it," he mourned to his father, and decided, then and there, that horse-trading was not for him. But, he asked himself, what was, then? Everything he thought of in the way of money-making, somebody else had thought of first. Every job he went after, somebody else already had. When, by chance, he happened to get one in a grocery store, his father made him quit the minute he found out that the foxy owner was cheating his customers by mixing cheap coffee with the best grade, and charging top price for it. Pa, and his honesty! Meanwhile Jim knew that his shoes had taken their last re-soling.

Chapter Three

A Lesson in Tolerance

Except for cash to buy his few clothes, Jim had little need for money. Like the neighboring farmers, the Penney family lived off the land. Jim had churned the family butter, and milked the family cow before he was eight years old. His sister cared for the chickens, and eggs came warm from the nest. Ma made the family bread, and canned and preserved vegetables and fruit from their own land. Bluegrass Farm slaughtered its own meat, and smoked and stored it to provide food for the long, bleak winter months. It was a self-sustaining way of life in which hard, continuous work was taken as a matter of course.

Jim grew up a good worker. Before he was twelve, he had learned to plow so straight a furrow that even his exacting father could do no better. Manure-spreading, corn gathering, haying, harvesting, he had done his fair share of them all.

He had nothing against farm labor. Indeed, he found real joy in working with his hands—a joy he was never to lose throughout his long, rich, rewarding life. Yet, now in his early teens, Jim had a growing conviction that he did not have the same feeling for the land as did the rest of the family; that he was not cut out to be a farmer. He secretly wished he could make a living some other way. He was only half way through high school. Perhaps by graduation time he might think of something with a more promising future for him than farming. If only, he sighed, he could do better in his school studies!

Although Jim had suffered his share of childhood sorrows, he was fourteen years old before he knew the anguish of a deep inner wound that never really healed until he was a grown man.

It made it so much harder to bear because it was inflicted by members of the little church which his father had served, as lay preacher, for twenty years, traveling the fourteen miles to it by horseback or buggy, in fair weather and foul, sometimes when he was so ill himself that he should have been in bed with a doctor in attendance.

Jim knew how dear to his father's heart was the little Log Creek Church, nestled in its grove of oak trees; how he farmed all week, looking forward to bringing the Gospel to his little flock on Sunday, using his scant leisure to prepare a sermon, or to visit the sick or dying, when the need was. He received no pay for this. As James Cash Penney, farmer, saw it, this was one way to live his religion.

Jim's parents were unusual members of the church and the community. They were educated. His father was a graduate, at seventeen, of a Missouri college. His mother was the daughter of well-to-do Southern parents, and had received every educational advantage it was possible to provide for a young lady of pre-Civil War days.

So, as well as their pioneering fortitude and devout religion, they brought with them to the Missouri frontier their education and cultural background.

Throughout the struggling years they had stood stoutly for education and religion. James Cash Penney believed in Sunday schools; that men should be educated for the ministry; that they should receive stipends for their services—and he lost no opportunity of saying so!

This to many Primitive Baptists of that day was not only radical thinking; it was rank heresy. They were bitterly opposed to having their children attend Sunday school, for fear they might be exposed to doctrines not taught by their own sect. Then, too, a church school, they argued, could easily become a threat to political freedom. All children should be taught the Bible by their parents.

Also, what was all this nonsense about a man needing special education to be a preacher? Any fellow with get-up-and-go, and God in his heart, could fill a rural church pulpit.

There were few Theological Seminaries in those days. Most of the little log churches in the vicinity had lay preachers. And as for being paid for preaching and praying! Why, that was unthinkable!

Farmer Penney had always liked debating. He

thought it was fine mental exercise; and these were church matters that Christians needed to think about and discuss.

The morning service was over that Sunday, and the congregation had eaten a picnic dinner under the oak trees, and now had assembled for the afternoon meeting. As he had done on other occasions, the Reverend James Penney brought up the controversial subjects, and stated his convictions regarding them.

And, as on former occasions, some agreed with him, some with the leader of the opposition—John Thompson, James Penney's nephew.

There had been several heated arguments before, but suddenly this one steamed to a boiling point. Thompson turned bitter eyes on his stiff-necked Uncle James who so stubbornly stood for these dangerous innovations. Scoffed Thompson, "If the church without these things, was good enough for James Cash Penney's father, who was my grandfather — and before him, my great-grandfather, who was also a minister of the word of God, according to the Primitive Baptists—then it should be good enough for James Cash Penney."

There was a murmur of approval from those who agreed with Thompson. By this time, teen-age Jim, who was not averse to a little argument to liven up a church meeting on a drowsy Sunday afternoon, grew scared. The air seemed charged with electricity, as before a big storm. He looked fearfully at his father's set, determined face.

Then cousin John was on his feet, vehemently demanding that his uncle be read out of the church, excommunicated by the congregation until he changed his heretical views.

Jim felt all the color drain from his face, as horror swept through him that anyone should dare to treat his father so. Through tears of rage and pain, he saw his father rise to his feet, to say calmly, "I have stated my views. I will not compromise them. Rather than cause any division in this congregation, I will leave now."

They had not mentioned excommunicating his wife. They had no wish to. In a second she was on her feet beside him.

"I believe as my husband does," she said firmly. "You can put me out, too."

Jim followed them down the aisle, through the old church door, to the waiting buggy under the oaks. He was numb with the hurt of this indignity done to his father, the injustice of it, the harshness.

They drove the fourteen miles back to town in silence. At last it was broken by his father. He looked down at his wife, smiled at her and said quietly, "Thank you, Mary Frances, for standing by me."

Monday morning, the farm work went on as usual. But not for Jim. The incident had shaken him to the depths. He seethed with inner fury. He could not understand his father's serenity in the face of such treatment. One day he caught his father's eyes on him, discerning, disturbed. "Jim," he said gently, "don't harbor bitterness. People see things as they see them. It takes time for ideas to take hold."

But the bitterness stayed. It was twenty years before Jim could set foot in that church again.

Of those mid-teen years, J. C. Penney says, "I felt out of place in the world around me, ill at ease. At school, I was only an average student. At games I didn't hold my own very well, being undersized. I wasn't often invited with others to parties. Schoolmates made fun of my clothes. I had to buy them myself and they were the best I could afford."

Perhaps all this rolled over the lad one summer evening as he sat beside his father on the back porch of the little home in Hamilton. That morning, they had driven in the two-wheeled cart the two and a half miles to the farm, and now, after a long, back-breaking day's work, they were back home, spent and silent, sitting in the warm twilight, resting.

All was still, save for the whispering of a breeze in the trees. His father was lost in thought.

The silence was broken by Jim. "I don't believe there is any God," he blurted out; then waited for a sharp reprimand. None came; only continued silence. Jim shot an inquiring look at his father's plain, stern face, and was surprised to see a sudden gentleness there, understanding, a trace of sadness and anxiety.

"Jim," he said, "prisons are full of men who don't believe in God."

Chapter Four

Challenged by the Golden Rule

Jim was seventeen when he was graduated from high school. That spring, as a pre-graduation gift, his father had granted him the use of four acres of land, telling him that he could grow what he liked, sell it, and keep whatever money he made.

"What shall I grow, Pa?"

"That's up to you, Jim."

Jim squirmed uncomfortably on the porch. That was the trouble with his father—always making him think for himself.

He considered one crop after another; then he thought of the watermelons. His father was expert at growing them, knowing about all there was to know in that field—the right seed, planting, cultivation, spraying and harvesting. Jim plied him with questions, to all of which his father's answer was a shake of his head.

"Pa, aren't you going to give me any advice?"

"Not unless you pay me for it, Jim. When you get

out in the world, you won't get professional advice for nothing. You'll have to pay for it."

"I don't think I want to pay you, Pa."

"I thought not. Good! Now you will learn by your own experience, not mine. I have loaned you four acres of good ground. The rest is up to you."

There was nothing for Jim to do but shoulder the responsibility, begin planting on his own. Was learning to be always a part of earning? It seemed that way.

He planted watermelon seed in his acres, knowing that this was only the start of his labor. As the new plants broke through the ground, he was there to hoe the soil around them. Soon his melon patch was green with vines, and in due time watermelons were thick on the vines.

Good fortune at last! He had a bumper crop. As his melons ripened, he was worried to see how many mysteriously disappeared. Thieves! He must guard them until they were ready to harvest.

As that great day grew near, he spent all night out in the field, with his dog and a gun. It was lonesome in his little tent, and chilly, and the dark hours dragged by. His eyes were heavy for lack of sleep. So much one had to put up with to make a living on a farm! Look at Pa, worried again about debts.

Just then his dog growled. Quickly he silenced it, and then held his breath to hear what the dog had heard. Yes . . . there was a rustle among the vines, and there, dimly seen, were two furtive figures slinking toward his biggest melons.

Now was the time to shoot! Jim pointed his shotgun into the air, and pulled the trigger once, then again. His shots in the still night air sounded to him like blasts from a cannon. They scared the thieves, too. "Don't shoot! Don't shoot! Jim, it's just us!" yelled the fleeing figures, running for their lives, with their empty hands held high over their heads.

Jim guessed they were some of the men who worked in the small bituminous coal mine in a corner of the farm, and which his father leased out on a royalty basis of five cents a ton. That ended the melon crime wave on Jim's four acres.

The season that had been a good one for Jim's venture had also been good for other growers of watermelons. They, too, had bumper crops. Jim faced up to stiff competition. He borrowed a horse and wagon from his father and began to peddle his melons from door to door in the streets of Hamilton. "Ten cents for the big ones," he told the housewives, "and a nickel for the smaller ones. Fine melons, ma'am. I grew them myself."

They surely were fine melons, and he sold a lot. But not enough. He still had too many left. Where could he find more customers? As he made his slow progress from door to door one Saturday morning, the answer came to him in a flash. Why, at the county fair, of course! This was the big day, and the people would be flocking there in crowds. He could park his wagon near the entrance, and sell his melons to the fair-goers.

No sooner said than done. Taking his cue from the noisy barkers inside the fair grounds, he began to shout, "Here they are, folks! Fine big watermelons! Sound and sweet and juicy! Big ones, ten cents; good ones for half a dime! Get 'em, folks! Get 'em right here!"

He was so busy handing out melons, making change, crying his wares, that he did not at first notice what others saw—his father, standing by the wagon, a look of mounting anger on his face.

Jim had seen that look before. He snapped off his spiel, waiting for his father to speak. Which he did immediately in cutting tones, "Jim, go home at once. You're a disgrace to the family!"

A hot flush of shame and indignation dyed Jim's face scarlet. That he should be reprimanded—treated like a naughty child — before this crowd of people, many of whom knew him! He smarted at the injustice of it, the humiliation. What had he done wrong? Was it a sin to sell farm produce to fair-goers? If so, he was in good company, for there were plenty of their neighbors doing it. What was wrong with making a little money? Wasn't that the reason his father had lent him the land on which to grow the melons?

His mind in a turmoil of fury and frustration, he drove his load of unsold melons home, and there awaited his father.

He did not have long to wait. James Cash Penney lost no time in informing his son why he had ordered him home. He had been guilty of unfair dealing, and he should have had the sense to know it, without being told!

Unfair? How was that? He had given his customers good value for their money.

Carefully, almost painfully, James Penney explained to his rebellious son what he had done that was so wrong.

"Have you ever heard of concessions, Jim?"

"No," muttered Jim, sullenly, his voice dull with despair.

"Didn't you know that people who sell things inside the Fair Grounds have to pay a fee to do so? Didn't you know that this is one of the ways a fair pays its expenses?"

Jim knew nothing about concessions. But he did know that there was no need for him to pay one.

"I wasn't inside the fair, Pa. I was outside."

"That's where your unfairness came in. By taking your stand outside the fair, and selling your melons to the public, without paying a tax or concession, you were being unfair to the people inside who had paid their tax. You had not paid for the privilege on a par with them."

"I was only trying to make a little money," protested Jim.

"You are entitled to make a living, Jim, but never by taking advantage of others. I thought I made that clear to you years ago, when I insisted that you get rid of your pigs."

Others! Always others, Jim thought bitterly. Respect the rights of others. Always be fair to others. How about being fair to your own son?

"I didn't know anything about concessions, and having to pay for them."

"So you said before. But that's no excuse. Just as ignorance of the law is no excuse for breaking it. And you certainly know now."

Jim's gray eyes were dark with misery and despair as they rested on his unsold melons. Why was his father so particular about all his family being what he called true and just in all their dealings? Other fathers might tell their sons, "Make money—honestly, if you can. But make money!" But not his father. He said, "Make money—honestly." Never that "if."

His father was looking at him now so intently that Jim's unhappy eyes were drawn to meet his steady gaze. "Don't ever let me see a son of mine take advantage of others for his own benefit. Think about it, Jim."

"Yes, sir," muttered Jim, never guessing how often he would recall this advice as he climbed up the ladder of success to become a millionaire merchant prince.

His father had more to say. "When I'm gone, Jim, if people passing my grave can say, 'Here lies all that is mortal of an honest man,' I couldn't ask for anything better. It's the finest thing a man can have remembered about him."

"When I'm gone!" Jim shuddered away from the very thought. Integrity . . . honesty — that was his father's way. "It's the way he wants me to be," sighed Jim, and went back to his unsold watermelons.

Chapter Five

Jim's First Job

Jim's late teen-age years were unsettled, far from happy ones. After his graduation from High School, people kept asking him, "What are you going to do now?" He didn't know. His brother, Elie, and his sister, Mittie, had their own farms. But he had no future in view.

He had a vague notion that he would like to be a lawyer. He was giving some deep thought these days about such subjects as the difference between right and wrong; honesty and cheating; fair play; respecting the rights of others—all these things that his parents found important. And he and his father had whiled away many a long winter evening debating some sizzling topic, suggested by his father. Wasn't all this good training for a fellow who felt the call to be a lawyer?

But he shrugged off the dream, knowing that he had never been a good student, his mind forever wandering off to ways and means to earn a nickel.

His father could not afford to send him to college,

and an uncle, when approached regarding a loan, had felt the investment too risky.

"Jim," his father worried one evening, when he was feeling far from well, "I just don't know what's going to become of you. The land has all been taken up."

Jim knew it was so, even though adjacent farm land had jumped from nine dollars to one hundred dollars an acre. He made no reply. How could he tell his father, now so sick and tired, that he did not want to be a farmer? He had liked selling his pigs and his watermelons. But as for the rest of the farm work, it had become just a necessary chore. If only he could find work he really enjoyed doing!

Things were not going well on the farm. It was still heavily mortgaged, and it seemed that no matter how hard and long his parents worked, they ended each year in debt. It probably need not have been so had James Penney been able to bring himself to plow up some of his acres of bluegrass, and plant them to corn, to fatten his stock for the market. As it was, he had to buy his corn, and this made the difference between profit and loss.

This odd quirk in the make-up of an otherwise practical farmer—this inconsistency in one who hated all waste, and labored ceaselessly to make both ends meet—was forever a mystery to all the substantial, down-to-earth people around them.

Perhaps his wife, Mary Frances, was the only one who understood her husband's inordinate love for his sweeping acres of bluegrass—a love so great that he carried in his pocket at all times a knife with which he could dig out any weed he found marring its beauty.

Mary Frances, a Kentucky belle, had been on a visit to relatives in Missouri when the first rumblings of the Civil War had so alarmed her parents that they had written for her to return at once.

No young lady, in those days, could travel alone. An escort must be provided. The choice fell on her cousin, James, son of the Reverend Eli Penney, a hardy Kentucky pioneer who had migrated to Missouri.

Young James, having brought his charge safely to her home, stayed on to visit. Here, on the bluegrass slopes, he found a different world—a way of gracious living, sheltered, carefree. Mary Frances, so unlike the daughters of pioneer farmers in Missouri, had never done a day's hard work in her life; had never cooked a meal. Her hands were smooth and white, her dainty gowns those of a young lady of luxurious leisure.

Mary Frances had been educated at a select boarding school before returning to her stately, white-pillared home to enjoy the social round of the Old South —horseback riding, neighborhood frolics, teas, dinners.

James fell deeply in love with his pretty cousin, Mary Frances Paxton, and wooed and won her. Was his bluegrass a symbol of that rare victory? Of a sweet romance he wanted to live forever in his memory?

A few honeymoon years in the soft living of the Old South, and then the young couple followed a mutual urge to go back to Missouri and face the rigors and the challenge of pioneer life.

Would a Southern belle measure up to the challenge? J. C. Penney tells how magnificently she rose to it. "In helping my father to establish a home in that raw, undeveloped country," he says, "she willingly took up her share of the burden. This included not only housework but some of the farm chores as well. Children came close together—and although it was necessary for her to do the work of two or three women in caring for the family and helping my father, never did I hear one word of complaint from her. No matter what new difficulty struck at our home, she met each new circumstance with a smile; with the calm assurance that there would be a way out."

The way out for Jim came with surprising suddenness when he was nineteen years old. His father was ill. After the Log Creek Church rumpus, his father entered politics, running for Congress on an Independent ticket. He had been defeated, and now was exhausted, seemingly unable to make a comeback to his usual good health and spirits.

Yet he left his sick bed to find a job for Jim. He had by now reluctantly accepted the fact that this so-different son was not cut out to be a farmer. It could be, then, that he had in him the makings of a good merchant.

Where better to start than at the dry goods store of the Hale Brothers, the outstanding merchants in Hamilton? James Penney held J. M. Hale in high esteem, both for his business ability and his integrity.

So one fateful Saturday morning in January, 1895, father and son set out for the store of J. M. Hale and

Brother, the father weak from illness, the son scared but hopeful.

Mr. Hale was surprised to see the ailing farmer out on such a bleak day. What could he help him with?

"Mr. Hale," said Farmer Penney, coming to the point at once, as if conscious that there was little time to lose, "will you take my boy into your store and teach him the fundamentals of honest business? He's a hard worker, and I've noticed he takes to selling."

Mr. Hale had all the help he needed. Moreover, February was always a dull month. Still, he had a great respect for upright James Penney, and would like to accommodate him by giving his son a start. He explained that he couldn't afford to pay an extra clerk much. That didn't matter, James Penney assured him. The important thing was not what Jim earned here, but what he learned.

Mr. Hale liked that. "Tell you what I'll do," he agreed. "If the boy wants to learn what he can of the business while he makes himself generally useful, I'll give him twenty-five dollars for the rest of the year of eleven months."

That would be two dollars and twenty-seven cents a month. James Penney was satisfied. The more money-minded Jim was not so sure. He could have earned twenty-five dollars a month driving a delivery wagon. But what could he learn doing that?

Jim went to work at Hale's store February 4, 1895, determined to learn all there was to know about selling dry goods, sure that at last he had found work that he could enjoy doing. He intended to be the best salesman in the store of J. M. Hale and Brother.

Not if the other six clerks, all older and more experienced than he, could prevent it! It was the custom in those days to put a greenhorn employee through a systematic, merciless hazing, and Jim, in his poor, ill-chosen clothes he had pinched pennies to buy, was an easy target. Sneering at his appearance, they nicknamed him "Mose." When they were not making slurring remarks about his clothes, they were ridiculing his small salary. "He's a very well-paid clerk," they would say with biting sarcasm. "He earns all of two dollars and twenty-seven cents a month. One of these days, he's going to be a rich man!"

Or it was his youth that convulsed them. "Mr. Hale isn't hiring men these days. He's hiring boys. This one, Mose, isn't out of his baby clothes."

"You'll never make a sale, looking the way you do," they would sneer; and should he get an occasional customer, one of the older clerks would brush him aside, saying, "Mr. Hale wants me to serve this customer. He's afraid you might lose the sale, since you know so little about the store."

There were days when he felt that he could not take it any longer; that he must quit. But then his family would have to know. No; he must keep all this from his father who wasn't getting any better.

Then one sorrowful day his weeping sister came hurrying to the store to ask if Jim could come home at once. The doctor warned that their father was sinking fast.

All the children were gathered around his bed, and he had a parting word for each. When his weary eyes rested on Jim, he smiled at him, and said to the family, with quiet confidence, "Jim's going to make it. I like the way he's started out."

Those were the last words Jim heard his father say. He died next day.

Chapter Six

Jim Hears Bad News

Says J. C. Penney, "It was rather freely said in Hamilton after Father's death that he left to his wife and six children his blessing, an upright example, and two mortgages—one on the stock farm and the other on the Hamilton homestead."

But the poor farmer-preacher had left to his son, Jim, a priceless spiritual legacy in the words from his death bed, "Jim will make it; I like the way he has started out."

Poor young Jim clung to those words as he battled against a terrible fear that he wasn't going to make it; that at the end of his first year, Mr. Hale would fire him because he wasn't earning even his meager salary of two dollars and twenty-seven cents a month.

The reason for his poor showing in sales, he was sure, was not that he lacked the ability to sell. It was simply that he rarely got the chance. The other clerks saw to that. Should he approach a customer, one of them would dart up and say, "Jimmy doesn't know the stock yet. Let me wait on you."

Time after time it happened, week in, week out. Then, as soon as Mr. Hale had left the store, they would begin their needling of him, their belittling.

Years later, when asked why they had put young Jim through this vigorous hazing, they had a ready excuse, "We wanted to make a man of him."

After a few months of having one customer after another stolen from him by the older clerks, Jim gave up trying to sell, and began busying himself sweeping floors and sidewalks, sorting, dusting and keeping the stock in neat order, running errands, making himself generally useful. Being a good chore boy—but not a clerk!

His father had liked the way he had started out. But as the months slipped by, Jim knew he wasn't getting anywhere. He was learning the stock, it was true, but he wasn't selling. Mr. Hale expected him to sell, and he was allowing the six older clerks to so be-devil, intimidate, and confuse him that he was headed for failure.

Then one day he seemed to hear his father's voice warning him, "Jim, you're not making your way here. At the end of the year, Mr. Hale will surely let you go, unless you start selling."

Until that moment, Jim had meekly taken whatever the other clerks had meted out. He had retreated before their jibes to the back room, where he had quietly gone about the tidying of counters and stock, making no attempt to meet and serve customers.

But now, at the thought that the unfair tactics of the other clerks might make him lose his job, fury seized him. How could he tell his mother, struggling to pay off the mortgages, and with three children still at home to provide for, that he had not been able to keep the job his father had risen from a sick bed to find for him?

Fear still gripped him. But something bigger now took hold of him. He knew he must face them, fight it out—or give up the struggle. Quit? "Never!" he gritted.

Standing at a counter in the rear of the store, he pounded it with his clenched fist, declaring wrathfully, "They're not going to stop me! They're not! I'll show them!"

And at that moment there came to him a spine-tingling realization of himself as a person—one in whom lay the power to succeed.

He strode forward to the front of the store, met a customer coming in, waited on her, and glowed with a sense of achievement.

As his own self-respect and spirit became apparent, the attitude of not only the other clerks changed toward him, but also that of Mr. Hale, who later said to him, "Jim, at first I didn't think you were going to make it. I had been watching you to see if you'd quit, or fight. I'm glad you didn't quit."

From that day on, Jim took his rightful place in the store. He liked people, and they liked him. All those trying months when he had found refuge in the back room of the store had given him a thorough knowledge of the stock, so that he could tell grade, weight, and price by the feel of it. He found selling a thrill, and no trouble too much to please a customer.

At the end of his first year, in spite of starting so late, he ranked third in sales, and Mr. Hale called him aside to tell him how pleased he was with his work, and that his salary for the coming year would be raised to two hundred dollars.

Jim could hardly believe it. To have started out at two dollars and twenty-seven cents a month, and in a year—and such a year—to have this increased to eighteen dollars a month! He was so shaken by the good news he could hardly get out a broken, "Thank you, sir."

The instant the store closed he hurried home to tell his mother. He worried over her, knowing that she was working too hard, trying, in addition to caring for the fatherless little ones, to pay off the debts.

When her husband died, the local banker had urged her to let the farm go for the debt, since its worth was not equal to the mortgages. But she would not listen to that. "I guess," she told him, "we'll pay our debts in the honorable way."

The banker had looked at her, aghast. Ridiculous! Never in her life had this woman had any business experience. Did she not realize that the total amount of this indebtedness was staggering? That to assume the gigantic task of paying it would seem an impossibility, even to a businessman accustomed to dealing in matters of finance?

His mother had nodded a serene head, said a secret prayer to God for help and guidance, and set to work. She made a garden to supply food for her growing children; baked bread to sell to the neighbors; sold milk from a cow she milked herself. And she squirreled away every penny she could save for payments on the mortgage.

Jim's pride in her courage was so deep that he could find no words to express it. But now, he rejoiced, he could help her more, with his two hundred dollars a year.

Breathless, he told her of this wonderful increase in salary. "I wish I could tell Pa," he sighed.

"I think he knows," said his mother softly.

Jim now threw himself into his work, eagerly waiting on customers, or listening to all Mr. Hale had to tell him, knowing that he must learn as well as earn. And at the end of his second year, Mr. Hale offered to pay him three hundred dollars. Another raise!

That was big money for those days, more than boys of Jim's age, in Hamilton, were earning. Jim was determined to more than earn every penny of it. He came to the store early, and stayed late. He drove himself so hard that before the year was half gone he was forced to see a doctor.

It was bad news. "Jim," warned the doctor, "you must quit your job at Hale's at once, and get out in the fresh air."

Jim stared at him, dumbfounded. Why, all he had the matter with him was this persistent bronchial cold!

"I can't quit," he said, flatly.

"You must," insisted the doctor. "You must get out of this Missouri climate at once, and go West."

At his words, a terrible fear clutched at Jim's heart. He could hardly bring himself to say the dreaded word.

"Do you mean that I have . . . tuberculosis?"

"Not yet, Jim. But it wouldn't take much more. My advice to you is to go to Denver. Right away! That is the advice I shall give your mother regarding you."

With a heavy heart, Jim took this frightening news to his mother. "You must do as the doctor says, Jim," she told him. "And don't worry about us. The Lord never leaves His children defenseless."

It was a hard break for Jim—to leave the farm he had helped to make, and his beloved mother, to whom he had grown even closer since his father's death.

He said a regretful farewell to his friend, Mr. Hale, feeling his eyes flood with tears at his words, "I hate to lose you, Jim."

As he looked back at the store, wondering when he would see it again, he little thought that twenty-eight years from then, he would return to buy it as the 500th link in his ever-growing chain of J. C. Penney stores.

Chapter Seven

Honesty's the Best Policy

Going West! As the train rattled along, Jim's mind seemed to shake with it, in a turmoil of emotions. He looked from one thing to another in the coach, as if to be sure that this was no bad dream. He dug his thumb in the red plush seat; stared back at the round glass container in which tepid water swished this way and that; steadied the box of food his mother had packed for him, so that he would not be hungry during his long trip.

A lump came to his throat as he recalled with what loving care she had packed in that box a whole roasted chicken, a loaf of brown bread, sandwiches, cake and fruit.

It hurt him to think that just when he had made the grade at Hale's, and was earning enough so that he could help her pay off that heavy mortgage, this blow had to fall. Who would have thought that a bronchial cold could so suddenly change the whole pattern of his life?

"What kind of a job can I get outdoors?" he worried. "I don't like farming, and all I know is drygoods."

Once again he was confronted with the urgent necessity to earn money. He could make do with the clothes he had, but he must find work at once, in order to eat, and have a roof over his head, for he had kept out only enough cash to pay his fare by coach, leaving with his mother all his savings of three hundred dollars.

The train lurched on, every minute taking him farther from the life he knew. He looked out at the acres of Kansas wheat, ripening in the June sunshine, and thought of his father's beloved bluegrass, and of the jackknife he had always carried in his pocket so that he could instantly cut out any trespassing weed. Father, who always wanted perfection in his work— and in Jim's.

Funny he should be thinking of bluegrass when all he could see from the glare of the train window was Kansas wheat! He was glad, he reflected, that his father in the last year of his life, had yielded to the pleas of his family, and allowed much of his bluegrass pasture land to be planted to corn. Jim smiled at the happy memory. A yield of 18,000 bushels at twenty-five cents a bushel! What a help that had been toward paying off the mortgages!

He hoped that the farm would do better now, with his older brother, and his sister's husband helping his mother to run it. They had a keener money sense than his father who had lived so much in a world of the mind.

The train whistled on with relentless speed, eating up the miles, as if anxious to toss Jim into the unknown West. Suddenly, his thoughts flashed back to that terrifying night when, as an eight-year-old boy, he had tossed in bed, frightened at the thought that from then on he must earn his own clothes . . . with holes in his shoes, and no job in sight.

He seemed to hear his father saying again, "You can do it, Jim. Just try. You'll find a way." He seemed to see his mother's warm smile again, just as she had twinkled down at his troubled face next morning, to assure him, "You'll think of something."

They had believed in him! Now his father was gone, his mother hundreds of miles away—and Mr. Hale was probably breaking in a new hand. Jim was alone.

"You're on your own! You're on your own!" the wheels of the lurching train seemed to taunt him.

The vast stretches of Kansas wheat gave way to the plains, and as the train sped over the parched land and dried-up rivers, the dust swept through the open coach windows to cover everything with grit.

"The doctor prescribed a dry climate," choked Jim, as, with the temperature well over 100, he tried to find something fit to eat in his lunch box, "and this is it!"

But with the first glimpse of the grandeur of the distant Rockies, and his first deep breath of the crisp, invigorating air as he got off the train in Denver, his spirits rose. Three generations of pioneers pulsed in his blood. Excitement mounted in him, and the call to something unbeatable that he knew was there.

He stood for a motionless moment in the busy station, as people looked with passing amusement at the figure he cut, clad in this hot June weather in a bulky overcoat that came well below his knees, carrying his overshoes, and with his bulging valise at his feet. A tenderfoot from the East, newly arrived. God help him!

But Jim did not notice their glances. He had one thought in mind—his immediate need to find a job. Lugging his heavy grip, his topcoat and his overshoes, he made a beeline for the business section, and stopped before a drygoods store. "If I could find work here," he told himself, "that would pay my room and board. Then I can look around in my spare time for that outdoor job the doctor said I must find."

Taking out his letters of recommendation, he handed them to the proprietor, who brushed him off. He had no time to read letters, he snapped, and what's more, he had all the help he needed.

Jim tried another drygoods store, and then another, and still another. The answer was always discouraging. Some needed no further help; others offered him such scant pay that even Jim, who asked so little, knew he would starve on it.

But Jim kept doggedly on with his job-hunting, and at last the proprietor of The Joslin Dry Goods Company offered him six dollars a week. Jim grabbed at it, then hunted a place where he could get room and board for four dollars and fifty cents, leaving him a dollar and a half for weekly spending money.

When he reported for work, he soon found that human nature was the same in Denver, Colorado, as in Hamilton, Missouri. Although at twenty-one, he was now too much of a man to be an easy victim of his fellow clerks' hazing, still he was a new hand, and the established staff combined to cheat him out of getting his fair share of the business. The head man was especially diligent in this respect. He was ever on his toes to prevent Jim from making a sale.

Fair dealing had been so drilled into Jim that each time a customer was snatched from him by the head clerk, he vowed it would be the last.

Then one day when Jim was showing eiderdowns to a pleased customer, and she had at last made her selection, the senior clerk stepped up to interrupt with a curt, "I'll finish waiting on this lady."

Jim held his wrath until the customer was out of the store. Then he confronted the suave senior clerk.

"That was my sale."

"I know it. What are you going to do about it?"

"Just this. If you ever do that again, I'll . . . I'll thrash you!"

The shocked senior clerk jumped, and gulped; then stared and sneered. But no more did he interfere with Jim's sales. Still, the social atmosphere of the store grew increasingly frigid, for it ill behooved the other clerks to seem not to be siding with seniority, and Jim decided to look for another job, and soon found one in Larimer Street.

Here, as Mr. Hale had taught him, he busied himself with becoming familiar with the stock, and while doing so he came across a mistake in marking goods, and immediately sought to draw the proprietor's attention to it.

"What is the correct price on these socks, sir?" he asked. "The price tag on those in this box is for twenty-five cents a pair, and for the socks in the other, two pairs for a quarter. Same grade of socks. There must be some mistake."

Jim glanced up to see the proprietor eyeing him strangely. "There is no mistake," he said, and turned away.

Puzzled, Jim explained, "But see, sir? They are the same quality."

"Young man," snapped the proprietor, "I'm paying you to sell things, not mark them. The price tags mean you're to get twenty-five cents a pair, if you can. If not, take some out of the other box, and sell them two pairs for a quarter."

"But they're exactly the same quality!" gasped Jim. "It . . . it isn't fair!"

Then the proprietor exploded. "You sell these socks the way they are marked!" he yelled. "And mind your own business! Don't try to teach me how to run my store!"

Jim felt sick all over as he went back to study the stock, and to find other articles marked with two prices. He remembered how his father had insisted on fair practices in all his business dealings; how Mr. Hale ran his store on the principle that honesty is the best policy. He needed the job desperately, but not enough to cheat customers.

That night he asked for his wages, and quit. Now he was jobless again. As he walked the streets of Denver he had time to think things through. He decided that Denver was not the place for him. It was too big. He liked small towns and small town people. They were his kind.

Jim remembered his father's statement that "no man could make a million dollars and stay honest." Was this true? Did most businessmen cheat in little ways, like in that sock deal?

"I never will!" he told the stars above him in the big city's night sky. "Some day, I'll have my own store, and I'll see that there is only fair dealing in it, both to my help and to my customers.

He trudged on, doing some hard thinking. "If I could only have my own store . . ." he dreamed. Then he laughed wryly. "Wake up, Jim Penney!" he told himself. "Why, you don't even have a job."

Chapter Eight

Testing an Idea

Within a few days—wonder of wonders!—he actually had a store of his own. As he watched his name, J. C. Penney, being painted in big letters under the picture of a bull's head on the window of the vacant, one-room shop, pride and joy surged through him.

He was doing what the doctor advised, he told himself, since this new job of his would take him into the open air as he visited nearby farms, looking at livestock.

For he had bought a butcher's shop. True, he was a drygoods man. But hadn't he grown up on a farm, helping his father to buy, raise and fatten stock? He knew little about butchering, he admitted. But that problem was already solved. He had hired a good meat cutter.

Jim took another deep breath of the bracing mountain air, thrilled to think that so soon after arriving here he was in business for himself. He was still a bit breathless from being whisked so fast from the big city of Denver, which he didn't like, to this little town of Longmont, which he liked very much.

It had all happened so suddenly, while he was still job-hunting in Denver. He had chanced to spot a notice of a butcher shop for sale in Longmont, about forty miles north. It could be bought for three hundred dollars, the exact amount of his savings, left with his mother.

He wrote at once, telling her of this fine opportunity he had of going into business for himself, and asking, if she could possibly spare it, to send him his savings. Without a moment's hesitation she had done this, and in a few days, the butcher shop had been his.

The farmer in him welcomed the prospect of chatting with nearby farmers, looking at beef cattle, calves, hogs, sheep, and buying what he needed for his butcher to dress for him.

For several weeks, all went well in his little one-room shop. The town people found they could get first-grade meat from the young man from Missouri, who kept his shop spotlessly clean, and was always warmly friendly and polite.

All his customers were satisfied but the chef of Longmont Hotel. He complained the new butcher wasn't sending his weekly bottle of whisky—the usual handout for his patronage. He aired his grievance to the meatcutter in no uncertain terms.

"You tell that young man if he doesn't come across with a bottle next Saturday, he'll lose the hotel trade!" he threatened.

Jim received the news with amazed concern. Wasn't he giving the chef his full money's worth? The finest selection of meat, the best service?

"Sure," agreed the meatcutter, "but unless you give him the whisky, he'll trade elsewhere. He's used to getting it. He's our best customer. We can't afford to lose him."

Jim bought the whisky, and took it to the chef. He knew he had a great deal to learn about the meat business. Perhaps this was part of it.

Then his conscience began to trouble him. As he tossed, sleepless, in his bed, the debate went back and forth, just as it had done in years past when his father and he had argued some sizzling question.

Reasoned Jim into the darkness, "Why should I object to whisky? Didn't my great-grandfather and my grandfather each keep a barrel of bourbon in their Kentucky cellars? And both of them ministers of the Gospel. They drank it in a gentleman's moderation, as a part of living."

Objected Jim's conscience, speaking in father's firm tones, "But I broke from that tradition. I saw the havoc wrought in human lives by strong drink, and I warned my children of the danger of it—you among them, Jim. You know my stand on this important question. What's yours?"

Poor harassed Jim didn't know. If he lost the hotel trade, he would lose the shop. If he lost that, he would lose his investment—his life's savings, accumulated chiefly by going without.

"I'll have to give it to him, Pa," he argued, tossing in his bed. "After all, what's a little gift to a customer?"

"Not a gift, Jim—a bribe."

"Pa, I've had it hard since I came West. Now, I've

got my first real start at making a place for myself.
Remember how you said on your deathbed, 'Jim will
make it'? I've hung on to those words. Pa, don't you
see that giving the chef the whisky will help me make
it?"

"That's not all I said, son. I said, 'I like the way he's
started out.' You started out at Hale's an honest boy."

Day after day Jim wrestled with it. Should he write
and ask his mother? But why waste time, effort, and
a postage stamp doing that? She would take her stand
by his father, as always. He could fairly hear her say
in her soft, sure way, "No whisky, Jim; no bribing to
buy or hold a business; no compromise with honesty."

Before the week was over, Jim had made up his
mind. He would buy the chef no more whisky; and
tell him why. The chef was not interested in explana-
tions. True to his threat, he withdrew the hotel trade,
and the inevitable happened. Jim lost his butcher's
shop.

Out of work again—and flat broke! In his walks in
the little town of about four thousand inhabitants,
he had been drawn to a drygoods and clothing store
that somehow reminded him of Hale's in Hamilton,
Missouri. It was owned by a T. M. Callahan, and Jim
heard that he and his partner, Gus Johnson, owned
several stores.

"If I could get a toehold in this store," Jim figured,
under his breath, "it might be my opportunity to get
ahead in work I know and like. I'd be satisfied with
small wages. It's the opportunity I'm after."

Jim stepped inside the store, and asked for a job.

"Give me just enough to keep body and soul together," he told Mr. Callahan. "I'll show you I can sell goods."

Mr. Callahan gave him a quizzical look. "We don't sell meat here," he said. "We couldn't use a butcher."

Jim felt his ears getting red. So news of his failure had gone abroad! Embarrassed, he blurted out, "I'm not a butcher, sir. I'm a drygoods man. I can prove it if you will give me a chance."

Mr. Callahan ran an appraising eye over the eager young job-hunter, now hopefully telling of his years of experience at Hale's, as he presented his references.

"I have all the permanent help I need," said Mr. Callahan, "but there is a vacancy you might fill until after the holidays. One of my clerks is home, sick. You might come on as temporary help until he returns."

Gratefully, Jim jumped at the chance, determined to do so outstanding a job that when the sick employee returned, Mr. Callahan would find his new hand much too useful a man to let go.

The busy, bustling holidays passed. Then Jim was kept on to help with the inventory. After that, the sick man returned, and Jim, worried at the thought of being one of the unemployed again, asked Mr. Callahan, "Shall I look for another job?"

Mr. Callahan did not answer at once. Then he said, as if still giving the matter thought, "Not if you would care to work for my partner and me in a store we have over in Evanston, Wyoming."

Jim's eyes shone with joy at the offer. "I'd like

that fine, sir," he said, "that is, if I can't stay on here with you."

Mr. Callahan began telling him about this Evanston store, and its unusual business set-up. It was, he explained, part of a special plan he had in mind—a plan by which he hoped to buy and operate a partnership chain of drygoods stores. Evanston was a trial link, as it were.

"Guy Johnson," he told Jim, "who is now manager of this Evanston store, used to work right here with me. A hard worker, eager to learn, and smart. As soon as I felt he was qualified for the job, I sent him to manage my new store in Evanston. And this is where my plan comes in. I sent Gus there as my partner, not my employee."

"Your partner?" puzzled Jim.

"Exactly; with a share in the ownership of the store, paid for from his savings from his job here. That way, his success is wrapped up with the store's, for he gets a third of the profit it makes."

Mr. Callahan's eyes, steady with the caution of experience, met the excitement in Jim's. "But," he went on, "a vital part of the plan is that now Guy, himself, must train his head clerk to be a manager, and do it just as thoroughly as I trained him. Then, when we agree that this man is ready, we will place him as manager of another new store, with Guy and me as his partners."

Jim listened intently, sensing even then the scope of this idea. He asked one eager question after another. Mr. Callahan did not pretend to have all the answers.

His plan was new, in its formative stage. It took studying, he said, to understand it.

But young Jim understood one thing fully. This partnership plan was the "seed" of a challenging fair deal, whereby a hard working clerk could one day become a partner in a new drygoods store, and progress from there to reach what might otherwise be an unattainable goal—the ownership of his own business!

"Yes, sir," he said, and his voice shook, in spite of himself. "I'd like to go to Evanston."

It would mean leaving his sweetheart, Berta Hess, behind in Longmont, but Berta, like his mother, always understood.

Chapter Nine

An Important Decision

After Jim had been junior clerk in the Evanston store for five months, and had saved one hundred dollars, he and Berta were married.

When Mr. Callahan had asked him if he would like to work for him in Evanston, Jim had been so excited about the offer, connected as it was with the electrifying idea of a chain of partnership stores, that he had quite forgotten to ask what his wages would be.

He learned on arrival that he was to get fifty dollars a month, and then decided that on that income, with the prospect of soon earning more, he could marry Berta Hess, the girl he had met and courted in Longmont. So he wrote to her, asking her to set the date, and on August 24, 1899, they were married in Cheyenne, Wyoming.

Now he had a heart-partner, a wise and willing helpmate in the tiny house where they had set up housekeeping—a girl as eager and ambitious as he for success, always ready to pack his supper in a tin pail, and bring it to him at the store should he stay late.

Which was often, for Jim was no clock-watcher. Indeed, the head clerk's favorite comment was, "Penney never knows when it is time to quit."

Cleanliness, neatness, thoroughness, and thrift had been drilled into Jim as a boy, his mother seeing to it that her children helped keep the house clean and neat; his father, that every corner of the farm was kept orderly and trim. This early training was now part of Jim.

When not waiting on customers, he gave the cluttered Johnson store a complete cleaning. Not a speck of dirt or dust would he tolerate. Much of the stock hung in festoons from the ceiling. Some of this he could display on hangers, or rearrange on counters or shelves to better catch the customer's eye.

He tried to put into practice all the things he had learned from Mr. Hale about good salesmanship, such as learning the stock; knowing exactly where everything was; and remembering the importance of selling the last two articles in a dozen lot, since all the profit was in these. "Anyone," Mr. Hale had impressed on him, "can sell new goods. It takes a real salesman to sell those last two."

Johnson approved of the way Jim was clearing the shelves of accumulated tail-ends. "Good merchandise," Jim said. "No excuse for it not to move."

There was no doubt about Jim's efficiency. Before he had been in Evanston a year, the mayor of the town approached him with a tempting business proposition.

"Jim," he said, "how would you like to have a store of your own?"

Jim could hardly believe his ears as the mayor offered to let him manage a store for him in a nearby town, making him a full partner, and paying him a monthly salary of one hundred dollars.

Jim's heart raced at the very thought! The very chance that he and Berta had yearned for—and at double his present salary! But then came that disturbing voice of conscience again. Would this be fair to Callahan and Johnson? To Mr. Callahan who had given him a helping hand when he most needed it? To Mr. Johnson who was his true friend as well as his boss?

"I couldn't make any decision without first talking it over with Mr. Johnson," he told the surprised mayor. "He's in the East right now, buying merchandise. When I've talked it over with him, I'll let you know."

Gus Johnson wanted to be fair, too. He reminded Jim of their plan to train young men to become partners in their business, and to have stores in a number of towns. That was in their thinking. But, for the present, he had nothing specific to offer.

"We would certainly want you to stay with us, Jim," said Mr. Johnson, "but the decision is up to you."

Was a bird in the hand worth two in the bush? Should he grab at the mayor's offer, and say "Goodbye" to Callahan and Johnson, the two fine men he worked WITH, not merely FOR?

At home, he and Berta talked it over, as they did all important business matters. They decided the right thing to do was to stay with Mr. Johnson. Jim told the mayor this, and went back to the store where he never knew enough to quit.

A few weeks later, Mr. Johnson called Jim into his office to tell him that they were opening a new store in the spring, and wanted him to manage it on a partnership basis.

"Thanks, Mr. Johnson! Thanks!" gasped Jim, and then began to worry about whether he had enough money saved to buy his share of the partnership. Would there ever come a time when he didn't have to worry about money?

"A store like this one?" he asked, his eyes going to where rows of shoe boxes reminded him that Callahan and Johnson had invested ten thousand dollars in shoes alone, to stock it. Jim had only five hundred dollars in his savings.

Johnson smiled his confident smile. "We plan to open a much larger store than this for you, Jim, in a much larger place. We're thinking of Ogden."

But Jim wasn't. He was thinking of some small town where lived the kind of people he knew best. Working people, miners, ranchers. Especially people who had to count their pennies, as he, himself, had always been forced to do. He knew what they wore, and liked seeing to it that they got the most for their hard-earned cash.

"Ogden's a big city," objected Jim.

"Sure. That's why I chose it for you. There are thirty-five thousand people in Ogden—all possible customers. Callahan is more like you. He favors the small towns. But not I. I contend that now that we're planning big things, we have to go to the big cities."

One busy Saturday afternoon, Johnson took Jim to inspect Ogden. The main street buzzed with business. Horses with saddles, horses harnessed to buggies, carriages, and wagons were as thick as automobiles are today. Up one side of the main street, down the other, the two merchants tramped. Not a thing escaped their keen scrutiny as they examined the window displays, and went into the stores to size up the stock, count the customers, and watch how the clerks handled all this business.

At every step Jim's spirits slumped lower as Johnson's zoomed higher. Later as they explored the town, Johnson was enthusiastic about this location for Jim's store. Look at all the city had—twelve churches, eleven hotels, five banks, a public library, a brewery, three parks, modern schools, telephones, and electricity—even an opera house, no less, seating two thousand people!

Jim's eyes searched the hordes of city shoppers, and didn't like what he saw. He had always looked on people as persons, never as the public.

They walked for miles, with Jim as silent as the grave. At last, Johnson lost all patience. "What's the matter with you, Jim?" he demanded. "Why don't you say something?"

Then Jim spoke. "I don't want to come here, Mr. Johnson. It's . . . it's too big."

Exasperated, the older man demanded, "Then where do you want to go?"

"To Diamondville."

"Ever been there?"

Jim admitted that he hadn't, but he had met a few of the people who lived there. They had traded in the Evanston store, and he liked them. "They're my kind," he told the annoyed Mr. Johnson. "They're ranchers and miners. We understand one another."

Johnson couldn't figure out why an ambitious young merchant could ever make such a foolish choice. He asked Jim his reason. And Jim gave it—one that made Johnson blink in bewilderment.

"I think," said Jim, "I could get closer to the people in a small place like Diamondville."

In later years, when J. C. Penney had a thousand stores and a thousand partners, when recalling this reply of his youth, he commented: "I never answered a question more truthfully or more spontaneously. There was every reason to think twice and make a canny answer to please Mr. Johnson, but I couldn't. . . . The man whom Mr. Johnson later placed in Ogden built a million dollar business. I have often wondered what my answer would have been had I been able to foresee a million dollars for myself. Probably my answer would have been the same, for when I look back and try to explain what there was in me that led to the growth of a nation-wide chain out of my first little store, I am inclined to put first this fondness for people, and especially for people like the miners and ranchers about Diamondville who are all there when you look into their eyes, without makeup or starched fronts."

The argument went on as Johnson and Jim rode back on the train to Evanston. Next week, when Callahan arrived at the store, he was met by Johnson's provoked, "Jim doesn't want to go to Ogden."

"Well," soothed Callahan, "it's a pretty big city."

"He wants to go to Diamondville."

Callahan and his partner made a trip to Diamondville, to look the place over. When they returned, Callahan told Jim, "That's not the place for you. Kemmerer is."

"Kemmerer?" questioned Jim, little dreaming that there he was to start what was to grow into the biggest store chain of its kind in the world. "Where's that? What sort of a place is it?"

Callahan told him that it was a lively little mining town not far from Diamondville, and suggested that he run up there and size it up for himself.

Jim wanted to—desperately. But the trip would cost him fifteen dollars. He decided that he couldn't afford it.

"I'll take your word for it that Kemmerer is the right place for me," he said.

Then, suddenly, Mr. Callahan was just as sure that Kemmerer was the wrong place for Jim. He had chanced to meet a business friend whose three sons had tried to operate a store there, and had failed. They were just as bright, their father maintained, as young Penney.

Now both partners were opposed to Jim opening his store in Kemmerer. Apart from their own financial risk in the venture, they did not want to see Jim fail. But, for some strange reason, stubborn young Penney still wanted to go to Kemmerer.

As a last resource, Mr. Callahan went to Berta and begged her to persuade her husband that Kemmerer was not the right place for him to open a new store, make a home for her, or raise a family.

"If Jim wants to go to Kemmerer—or, for that matter, to the top of the Wasatch Mountains—" she told Mr. Callahan, "I'll go with him."

That settled it! Mr. Johnson estimated that it would take six thousand dollars to launch the new store. His partners offered to lend Jim, at eight per cent, the fifteen hundred dollars he lacked for his one-third partnership. But Jim wrote to one of the banks back home, in Hamilton, and it agreed to lend him the money at six per cent.

"I saved thirty dollars," exulted Jim to Mr. Johnson, "and all it cost me was a postage stamp."

Chapter Ten

The First Penney Store

Jim and Berta arrived in Kemmerer, Wyoming, on April 1, 1902. It was a typical small western town of those days, its business section consisting of a few wooden buildings, mostly of one story or a story and a half. There was the usual wooden rail hitching post around the trading area. Before the vacant building which Jim had just rented for forty-five dollars a month, there still remained one of the early wooden sidewalks which was to defy all Jim's persistent efforts to sweep it clean.

When the young couple arrived in this bleak, raw mining town of about one thousand inhabitants, the winter was still in the ground, now soggy with mud. No trees or landscaping softened its stark crudeness. It was not a promising outlook.

Jim realized that Mr. Callahan did not think he could succeed here. Nor, evidently, did Mr. Pfeiffer, cashier at the town's one bank. He had only discouragement for Jim, warning him from his experienced viewpoint that no cash and carry store could do anything but fail in Kemmerer. For the simple reason that cash, among the miners, was so scarce as to be practically non-existent.

Jim was fully aware of the difficult situation. The miners in the town were supposed to buy supplies from the Company stores. Actually, the pressure on them to do so almost amounted to force and intimidation. When the miners were paid, they received part cash and the rest of their pay in script, or certificates for specified amounts to be used only in Company stores.

"The mining companies," explained Mr. Pfeiffer to the newcomer, "allow their workers to trade at stores that will sell goods on credit covered by these certificates which their employers then deduct from the worker's wages. Even the saloons accept these certificates. I honestly think you will not be able to do a cash business here, Mr. Penney. I most certainly would not advise you to open a cash and carry store here."

"I have already rented a storeroom," admitted Penney.

"Where?"

"On Pine Street—that vacant building beyond the triangle."

The cashier's face was the picture of stunned disbelief. That impossible place, two blocks from the station, between the Chinese laundry and a cheap boarding house! With not even water on the premises!

"Why, that is no location for any kind of a store," he protested, "least of all, a cash and carry one!"

But young Penney met his objections with a confident smile. If he had any secret doubts, he would not admit it.

"I believe, sir," he said firmly, "that you will be surprised at the amount of cash business we shall do in that little Golden Rule store."

The building Jim had rented might have discouraged a less intrepid soul. It comprised one small room on the ground floor—the store; and above it, what was to be their future home—an attic, reached by an outside stairway.

The attic was as bare as the store. It was lighted by the door, and a small window, no bigger than a porthole, through which tenants could draw up by a rope, pails of needed water, borrowed from the Chinese laundry. At first the attic's only furnishings were two articles purchased by Jim from his scanty funds—a bed, and a small pot-bellied stove, the latter their only source of heat and hot water.

But as soon as the merchandise began to come in, there were crates and boxes they could use for a table and two chairs. The time would come when Berta would wrap her baby son in old clothes, and tuck him snugly in a crate to sleep under the counter while she waited on customers.

The ground-level room in the building, the store, was just four walls, a floor, and a ceiling. There were no fixtures, and Jim had no money with which to buy any. But there were still plenty of empty crates in which the merchandise had been shipped. From these, Jim carefully drew out the nails, straightening the bent ones, and made shelves and a counter. One of those rough, early counters is now a treasured exhibit in the towering J. C. Penney headquarters in New York City. It is easy to imagine young Jim standing behind it, wrapping up some socks—"as cheap as two cents a pair"—in paper he has salvaged from the trash box, and neatly trimmed and then tying the package with used string he has thriftily unknotted to serve again.

With the date set for the opening store, Penney launched his initial advertising campaign. He had already obtained through his contact with customers from Kemmerer in the Evanston store, the names of five hundred miners. Now, he mailed to each a flier, announcing the opening of his new Golden Rule store, and proving by his listed prices that it would pay to trade there.

That done, he deluged the town with handbills, telling how people could save money by dealing at the new cash and carry store, which would open at sunrise on Monday, April 4, 1902. Not a doorstep was missed!

Never was Penney to forget that amazing opening day in the jerry-built, wooden building, with its crate and box furnishings, and the magic words, "Golden Rule," in large letters over the attic window. Many a time, after he had become a millionaire merchant-prince, he would recall that day with eyes wistful with memories.

The miners and ranchers poured in, from sun-up to midnight, eagerly examining the fresh, new wares, selected so obviously by one who knew their needs—and paying for them in cash. Berta worked steadily beside her husband, serving the miners' wives with a courtesy and warm friendliness that they did not find in the company stores.

The crowded hours flew by. When midnight came, the weary couple climbed the outside stairway to their attic home, carrying with them the cash from their first day's sale.

That was a thrilling moment! Locking the door, Penney lit the kerosene lamp. Then, sitting on their shoebox chairs, at their drygoods box table, they counted the pennies, nickels, dimes, quarters and half-dollars, and the very few bills. The total was four hundred and sixty-six dollars and fifty-nine cents, almost as much as the five hundred dollars savings he had invested in the store, to pay for his one-third partnership!

Jim looked at his wife, as bone-tired as he, and met her victorious smile. He knew that it would not always be as good as this. There would be dull times, when the miners were working only two days a week, and busy seasons when the ranchers could not spare their horses for shopping trips to town. He must not be too optimistic. Yet he anticipated with a degree of malicious joy the look on cashier Pfeiffer's face when he deposited all this cash money.

And after he had blown out the kerosene lamp, and stretched wearily in bed, before he closed his eyes in sleep, he thought he heard his father's voice, saying, "Jim will make it. I like the way he has started out."

In the months that followed, Jim and Berta worked from early morning to late at night. The store opened at seven, and was not closed at night until Penney had convinced himself, by going outside and surveying the empty street, that there was not the slightest chance of making another sale.

At first, Jim and Berta did most of the work, with Berta hurrying down from the attic to tend store while Jim ate his lunch and supper. Soon Jim, who had once tossed in his bed, worrying how he was ever going to buy himself a pair of shoes, was doing most of the community's shoe business, selling hundreds of pairs to miners.

It was necessary to keep the store open even on Sundays, since the miners worked six days a week, and it was the only day sheep ranchers had time to drive into town. This troubled Penney's conscience, violating, as it did, the teaching of his church and home. But there seemed nothing else to do.

And when on some Sunday morning, some trusting foreign-born miner would bring in a bewildered friend newly-arrived from the old country to be fitted out with his first American work clothes for his new job in the mines, Penney would have a deep sense of satisfaction, and as he helped the stranger get his full money's worth, he would remind himself that in all true work there is something of divineness.

At the end of the first year in his Kemmerer store, his sales reached nearly twenty-nine thousand dollars! Jim's share in the profits paid off his entire loan, and he was now a full partner, with no debts.

Chapter Eleven

The Partnership Plan Begins

In later years, J. C. Penney admitted with a twinkle in his eye, that in those early days at Kemmerer he must have been a hard man for whom to work. He insisted that his clerks keep busy, not fritter away spare moments in chatting, reading the newspaper, or just standing around. Weren't they being paid to work? Then, if there were no customers to be served, they should busy themselves cleaning and arranging the shelves, dusting, sweeping the floor—and that wooden pavement outside the store that seemed always in need of a broom.

It was generally agreed in Kemmerer that young Penney was a hard driver. He actually expected his help to work as hard as he did—and a man would be a fool to do that!

When Penney's name had become a household word, one of the early Kemmerer employees recalled how he and a fellow clerk had to work such late hours that the only way they could be sure of getting their

sleep was to spend the night in the store. For no matter how late Penney had kept the store open the previous night, he expected his clerks to have it swept out
and shipshape for business by seven in the morning.

"Within a month," he declared, "thirty-nine employees had quit that store. No one could stand the
work. Why, one day Mr. Penney walked in and found
two clerks sitting on the counter, eating apples. He
fired them both, saying he hadn't employed them to
eat, but to work. He was 'money-mad!' "

Penney thought about that accusation. The memory of the lack of money on his father's farm was still
with him. Most certainly he wanted to make money!
His salary as manager in those days was only seventy-
five dollars a month. To make money, he had to keep
down operating expenses to a minimum, buy carefully,
sell goods, build up his business, and get ahead on his
share of the profits. It meant slaving and saving.

"I want to make hay while the sun shines," he
wrote in one of his Kemmerer letters. "I am young,
and am anxious to fix myself so in my advanced years
I will have enough to keep me comfortable, and also
to provide amply for my wife and children, in case of
accident to myself."

And then, when he had time to think of it, there
was the Partnership Plan! If they were to have that
dreamed-of chain of drygoods stores extending through
the mountain states, then he must have the money
earned with which to invest in them.

At that time, in his wildest flights of fancy, he
visualized the chain as consisting, at the most, of six

stores. Even that, he sighed to Berta, was like shoot-
ing at the moon.

In his mind, there was beginning to shape up a picture of the type of man needed to insure the success of
the partnership plan; and in 1903 he was to find out, by
first-hand experience, the type that, however well
trained, spelled failure.

At the time Callahan and Johnson had sent Penney
to Kemmerer, they had sent another of their clerks
to operate one of their stores in Rock Springs. He had
been with them a long time, and knew his job. Yet,
for some unknown reason, the Rock Springs store continued to lose money. So Callahan and Johnson offered
Penney an interest in the failing store if he would go
and lend a hand there.

Penney soon found the trouble. The man in charge
had one eye on the store, and the other on the extra
cash he could make on the side, playing his trombone
in the town band. This meant rehearsals and evening
concerts.

The morning after one of these evenings, the musical manager would arrive late at the store, much too
tired to be alert or agreeable. After yawning through
the day, he would close the store early to attend another rehearsal.

Penney finally decided that a man of such divided
interests was not manager material, and let him go.
He replaced him with a man of his own choosing, and
the store was soon out of the red, and making a fair
profit.

This experience deepened Penney's conviction that

much of the success of the partnership plan hinged on finding the right men to serve as the living links of the chain.

The following year, Penney suggested to his two partners that they open a third store in the little mining town of Cumberland. He was happy that this time he did not have to borrow the money to pay for his one-third share in it. He was able to buy it with his Kemmerer earnings.

With three stores now to manage, his responsibilities grew. He was forced to spend more time away from home, buying merchandise and keeping close contact with the newer stores. He had less time for personal talks with Callahan and Johnson, so he was totally unprepared for the shock when, in 1907, they told him that they had decided to dissolve their partnership.

"We will sell you our interests in the three stores in which you have a share for thirty thousand dollars," they told him.

Penney felt his heart thumping within him. His dream had been to own his own store. Here was the breathtaking chance to own three. But the cost! Thirty thousand dollars! How could he borrow so large a sum? If he gave a lien on the stock in the stores as security, it would affect his credit.

Callahan and Johnson offered to lend him the full amount at eight per cent interest, and to accept his name on the note as their only guarantee of payment, and while Penney's head was still spinning with the wonder of it, the legal papers were signed.

As he shook hands with his old partners, he could hardly believe it. At 32, only seven years after he opened his first store in Kemmerer, Wyoming, he was the owner of three drygoods stores.

Now, more than ever, the problem of finding the right men to train and test confronted him. He mentally listed the required qualifications of a Penney trainee. He must be ambitious, eager to get ahead. He must be a hard, tireless worker. He must believe in God. He must not drink liquor. He must be willing to start at the bottom, seeing nothing menial in working with his hands—scrubbing, sweeping, cleaning windows. He must be willing to work long hours.

Above all, he must have an ingrained integrity to keep him true to the high principle by which the stores were operated—the spirit of the Golden Rule, insuring fairness to his employer, to fellow workers, and to the customer. Was that too much to ask of the man behind the counter?

Penney, himself, was now in need of a partner. The dream of an ever-growing chain of stores which Callahan and Johnson had left with him was now always in his thoughts. He and Berta would discuss it at the end of a hard day's work, at first as they sat around the stove in the attic; then in the little home across the street, which he had bought for five hundred dollars, and where their second son was born.

"Berta," Penney would say, a shining star of hope in his tired eyes, "it is going to be just as I planned. Some day you will see a chain of our stores all along the west coast."

"Why not a few in the East, too?" Berta challenged him one evening.

But her husband, for all his ambition, shook his head at that. Who, in all the world, he wanted to know, would want as many as that? After you had made just so much money, he pointed out, you wouldn't know what to do with any more.

Berta chuckled at the fantastic idea of having so much money that you didn't know what to do with it. Even though the boxes and crates had been replaced by chairs, and her second baby did not have to sleep in a wooden box padded with old clothes, yet they still lived with utmost economy, saving every cent they could.

It happened that while Penney was searching for an ideal partner, that man, although he did not know it, was searching for just such an opportunity as Penney had to offer in his partnership plan in connection with his add-a-store chain project.

The man was Earl Corder Sams. Like Penney, he was a farmer's son who preferred storekeeping to farming. He was experienced, and had a good position as manager of a general store in Simpson, Kansas, but could see no future ahead. He thought he might find it in the West.

He wrote to an employment agency in Denver, giving his qualifications, and asking if there were any openings there in his line of work. The agency informed Sams of the Penney Golden Rule stores where the opportunity for advancement was particularly good.

There followed weeks of correspondence, then an interview. Each man wanted to be quite sure he was not making a mistake. At times, the outcome hung in the balance, but at last Earl Corder Sams, his wife, and their little fox terrier came to Kemmerer, and for a week, Penney was filled with doubt. Could a man who alighted from the train carrying a little dog in his arms ever make a good manager?

But his fears were groundless, for Sams of Simpson served as Penney's loyal and efficient right-hand man for almost half a century, rising to be president of the J. C. Penney Company in 1917, and chairman of the board in 1946.

Chapter Twelve

The Loss of a Helpmate

It took only a few months for Penney to know that Earl Corder Sams was a man after his own heart, and had all that he was looking for in a partner. Half a century later, when he was giving one of his many speeches before organizations, J. C. Penney spoke thus of young Sams who came to work for him in his first store:

"He waited on customers, swept and scrubbed floors, washed windows, kept the stock clean, and when I was absent, milked the family cow. His hours were from 7 o'clock in the morning until 10 or 11 at night. His pay was seventy-five dollars a month."

After Sams had been a year in Kemmerer, Penney decided to send him as manager of the Cumberland store. This would be a real test of his ability to win out in a tough spot. Cumberland was a mining town, and its general store was operated by the company, which had forbidden Penney and his former partners to open their store in the town. So they had opened in a building just outside the city limits.

It was about the size of the Kemmerer store, but had no attic. Sams and his wife lived in two rooms back of the store. There were no conveniences. They had to get their water from a mountain stream about half a mile away. It was primitive living, but Sams and his wife were happy, stirred by the challenge of an interest in a store of their own—the "future" that they had left home to find.

They worked side by side in the store, as Penney and Berta had done in the early Kemmerer days. At the end of the year, by frugal living, they had saved almost a thousand dollars, whereupon Penney invited Sams to become a partner in a store in Eureka, Utah.

Sams did as well in Eureka as he did in the Cumberland store, and, with two other men trained and tested by Penney now managing two new stores in the chain, Penney began to talk to Berta of having not six, but twenty-five or even more stores, and men to manage them, and be his partners.

Sams was always in his thinking now. He sought every opportunity to explain his expansion plan to his busy partner. It might seem involved, he pointed out, but really it was simple.

"Briefly, it enables a store manager who has saved enough money out of his earnings to buy a one-third ownership in a new store, so that he can get into business for himself . . ."

"Provided . . ." put in Sams, reminding him of a very important proviso that had to be met, head on.

Penney shot a pleased, appraising look at him.

"Yes; provided he has trained a man capable of opening and managing the new link in the chain."

Sams was silent for several seconds, turning the plan over in his mind. Then he said, "What you are really planning is an organization that will always be renewing itself from within."

Penney nodded. It was more than that, but, at present, that was enough to be caught in words.

As the two men lugged mountain clear water from the stream to the Cumberland store, they talked shop all the way. Penney told how he was planning to invade Mormon country, in spite of the warnings he had received that the Mormons would not trade with Gentiles.

"I don't believe it," he told Sams. "I had Mormon customers in Evanston and Kemmerer. They're fine people, industrious, honest, and God-fearing."

Sams agreed with him. Mormons came to trade in his Cumberland store. "Honest themselves," he commented, "all they require of a merchant is that he be honest with them."

At that time, Utah, Wyoming, and the rest of the high country was still the frontier. Penney and Sams knew from experience the hardships and hazards of such trail-blazing as they were now planning.

Penney's idea was to by-pass big cities—he remembered Denver—and open his stores in small country towns of a thousand to three thousand population.

"I know how to run the sort of store that appeals to small town people," he explained to Sams. "I know how to select merchandise for them. I understand them, and they understand me."

Sams nodded. He was a small town man himself. He understood what Penney meant.

"What about these partners?" he asked. "Will you put them under bond?"

"Not if you mean a surety bond. They will be under a moral bond, like you. I intend to have as my partners only men of character, and that sort never break moral bonds. I don't want men who need a halter around their necks to make them do the right thing."

The two young businessmen talking so seriously on the outskirts of the little mining town of Cumberland had become close friends in one short year. The bond that held them was more than ambition, enthusiasm, energy, an inner drive, pushing them to the top. It was character; their belief in fair dealing.

"If you want to come in with me on this expansion plan, Mr. Sams," offered Penney, "you or I can put up the remaining two-thirds of the money needed to start each new store. Or, if you don't want to do it singly, we can do it together."

Sams soon showed how definitely he wanted to be part of the plan. He trained one manager after another to open new stores, so that by 1910, Penney had a chain of fourteen stores.

In 1909, Penney had given up managing the Kemmerer store personally, and had moved to Salt Lake City. His two little sons were now old enough to go to Sunday school, and the Penney family was attending the First Methodist Church, where the six-foot-four Dr. Francis Burgette Short was the minister. This many-sided scholar was to become closely associated with the educational program of the Penney Company in the years to come.

The eight years at Kemmerer had been strenuous ones for Penney and Berta. Now, with Sams proving so efficient a partner, Penney felt he dared relax. There had been no time for a honeymoon after their marriage. Why not take a belated wedding trip now? Perhaps to Europe!

Berta was thrilled at the very thought. "Couldn't we go to the Holy Land?" she begged.

Penney, the minister's son, who, oddly enough, had never joined a church, although he was a liberal financial supporter, smiled back at her. She had worked so hard during these difficult years, had been tied down so closely to the store. Now he was going to give her a taste of longed-for travel. Perhaps they could go to Bethlehem and Nazareth, the Sea of Galilee, the Garden of Gethsemane—walk where Jesus walked.

Maps were pored over, plans made to start right after Christmas. What a Christmas it was going to be! The tickets were bought, the luggage packed.

Then Penney had to make a last-minute trip to one of his stores. He hated to leave at such a time, but it was urgent.

Berta had been having trouble with her tonsils, and her doctor had advised her to have them taken out before starting on the sea voyage. She decided to get the operation performed while her husband was away, so that all would be in readiness when he returned.

Late one evening when Penney was working with a partner in one of his distant stores, there came a steady pounding at the door.

"So late?" said Penney.

"Maybe some farmer wants to buy something before he leaves town," said the store manager, hurrying to the door.

It was no customer, but a messenger from the telegraph office with a telegram for Penney. It read, "Come home. Your wife is seriously ill."

Terror clutched at Penney's heart. Quickly packing his briefcase, he hurried to the railway station, caught an early train, and in a few hours arrived home.

The doctor met him at the door. Penney's distraught eyes searched his face for hope.

"She has acute pneumonia," the doctor told him. "I am afraid she may not live through the night."

Berta died without knowing that her husband was at her side. That was Christmas, 1910.

Chapter Thirteen

Penney Learns About Life

His wife's death was a shattering blow to Penney. It seemed as if his busy world had come crashing down about him, leaving him crushed, bereft, and filled with a strange, unbearable loneliness. His grief-stricken eyes went from the luggage Berta had packed with such joy, to his two little sons who needed her so.

Had she been seriously ill for a long time, perhaps it would not have been such a cruel shock. But this simple little tonsil operation! It had been successful, and, after a few days at the hospital, Berta had walked home, and had been drenched in a heavy shower. She had become feverish, the neighbors said, and the family doctor had been called. Then, almost immediately, had come acute pneumonia—and sudden death!

Penney, his soul bruised and battered, recalled all the sacrifice and struggle of the lean Kemmerer years, and how cheerfully she had shared it all with him. And, now, when his business was at last assured, and he had money, and could, in a way, have made it up to her, it was too late.

Money! What was money when the one dearer than life to him was dead? What good had his money done her? He felt mocked by life—even by God.

He tried to take up his work again—to open new stores, and visit all the managers of those already in the chain. He pushed on with his plan to set up a system of centralized finance and accounting through which all the business of all the stores in which he had an interest could be cleared.

He went on doggedly with his personal pet project —the establishing in Salt Lake City of a large wholesale warehouse to which all his managers could come to select their merchandise, thus saving them the time and expense of their twice-a-year buying trips to New York City.

But all the thrill and adventure were gone. He told of it in a simple, stabbing sentence: "To go forth on new ventures and know that the understanding smile will not be there to approve of them, empties the world of all that is most precious in life."

His partners tried in vain to help. It seemed as if a curtain had been drawn between them and his grief.

"Why?" he kept asking himself. "Why did God let this happen to me? Haven't I lived by the Golden Rule? Haven't I established it in every new Penney store, encouraging, training, and financially helping my managers to share in what they have helped to create, and become owners of their own stores? Haven't I been just and fair in all my dealings? Why has God let me down?"

In his distraught state of mind, he siezed upon

every opportunity to leave the familiar surroundings that held too many sad memories, and go to New York on business trips. The day's official work done, he would walk the streets at night, seeking the city's shabbiest sections. He felt more at home with misery.

Then came a still more terrible thing to torture him —an unheard of, inexplicable torment. He who had never touched liquor in his life now had a driving desire to drink! The craving lasted not only months, but years.

Penney fought it desperately, knowing that he dared not yield to taking that first drink; that if he did, he would be lost. Sleepless, his nerves ragged, he walked New York's streets, night after night, battling not only his grief and black depression, but this new, hideous temptation that had fastened its evil clutches on him.

Sometimes his midnight walks led him to the Bowery where he saw the hopeless wrecks of men, the sodden drunks, asleep in dark doorways. At least, he thought bitterly, they could sleep.

Sometimes he walked the dingy streets of the lower East Side until he came to the river. There he would stand on some deserted coal dock, and search for an answer in the dark waters, which at times seemed to tell him that the solution was simple. All he need do was slip into them, and drift away. Suicide would be an easy way out—an escape from loneliness, and this incessant craving to drink.

One wintry night he set out to walk the city streets in the hope that sheer physical exhaustion must bring

him a good night's sleep. He was striding along the
Bowery, every step showing him more human misery
and depravity, when a strange sound struck his ears—
a fragment of an old hymn wafted through a crack of
a rescue mission door to wing its way into the dark
chill of the night.

"Jesus, Lover of my soul . . ." they were singing
inside the mission. The night wind was bitter, and Penney was very weary, having walked half across the
city. He pushed open the old door and sank down gratefully to rest in a back seat of the little mission hall.

The singing over, he was soon listening to the testi-
mony of a well-dressed man up front, who told how he
had been rescued from a drunkard's life by this mission which had picked him up from the gutter, fed and
clothed him, and found him a good job.

"I found Jesus here," the man said simply. "I had
never known Him before."

The redeemed drunkard's words rang in Penney's
ears as he retraced his steps. "Do I really know Him?"
he pondered, "the way that rescued man does? True, I
was brought up by religious parents, in a religious
home. I live and run my business by the Golden Rule.
I attend church. I give to many other good causes. But
is this enough? Do I really know Him?"

Penney fell asleep that night, fancying he heard his
father's confident, "Jim will make it."

Returning to Salt Lake City, Penney tried again to
lose himself in work. He opened new stores in rapid
succession. He saw the volume of sales zoom to amazing proportions. His business was growing by leaps

and bounds. For two hard-driving years, he gave his concentrated attention to its direction, but the feelings of loss and restlessness were still with him.

Often, at the end of a grueling day, his thoughts would go back to the trip abroad he and Berta had planned, but had not taken. Why not take it now? Get away from it all? His two sons, in boarding school, were old enough to accompany him, for Roswell was ten, and J. C. Junior, seven.

The minister of his church, Dr. Short, had been a real friend to him, especially during the past two sad years, so Penney now suggested that the scholarly clergyman join them on their trip to Europe, Egypt, and Palestine. An old friend of Penney's, a retired Evanston merchant, also accompanied them.

Penney was still asking "why?" The "why" of Berta's death; the "why" of the unrest and discontent within him; the "why" of the strange fact that although his manager-partner plan, and his dream of an ever-growing chain of Penney stores were successful beyond his rosiest expectations, yet he still had this gnawing feeling of lack, of an inner hunger.

Dr. Short proved to be a perfect companion, both on ship and shore. He was a widely-read and cultured man, and a strong, original thinker. Penney delighted in drawing on his superior knowledge of the Bible. There were quiet, deep, enlightening talks as they trod the paths that Jesus had walked in the Holy Land, and during one of them, Penney stumbled on a hard fact that made him square his spiritual shoulders. Simply this: IT IS USELESS TO RUN AWAY FROM LIFE.

"Life is life," he reflected. "Rough, as well as smooth; darkness, as well as light. In every life there is death. . . . I am going to stop running away from life-as-it-is."

The minister's son in him made him alert to every holy place of biblical history; the merchant in him, to the tragic lack of any means whereby goods could be distributed to the struggling millions who lived off the beaten track in the Near East.

He saw his chain in a sparkling new light—as a system of distribution that had a worthy place to fill in bringing goods to the settlers who, with the heart and courage and dreams of the pioneer, were building in the West the frontier towns where he and his associates were building stores. There was a touch of glory about finding the best possible goods, at the lowest possible price, for such people!

Three generations of pioneer blood flowed in Penney's veins. While he was in Europe, there were times when he sensed the massive pent-up urge which had literally driven great numbers of human beings to cross the Atlantic Ocean, and the Appalachian chain, daring prairies, desert, and mountain range, to break their bonds of slavery to outmoded social and economic ways.

"These were tillers of the soil," he wrote, "miners, farmers, herders—but, above all, they were freedom-seeking pioneers. Where they came, others are following. By their swift dispersion from narrow, archaic environments they are creating an incalculable demand for basic goods, over a territory that rivals the whole of Europe in area, and where as yet there are no modern facilities for bringing them goods of quality in quantity."

Penney, the dreamer, became Penney, the practical businessman. He glowed as a new realization dawned on him of the tremendous possibilities that were his through his chain of drygoods stores, to play a major part in supplying this incalculable demand for basic goods. As the great ship sailed homeward, Penney thought and planned . . . thought and planned, his keen mind busily devising new ways of strengthening and developing the organization for greater service.

Back in America, rested and relaxed, and eager to get back into harness, he found that his unique partnership plan had gone on working without him, so that now thirty-four Penney stores were flourishing in eight Western states—two in Wyoming, thirteen in Utah, seven in Idaho, two in Nevada, two in Oregon, three in Washington, four in Colorado, and one in Montana.

Chapter Fourteen

Penney's Program for Growth

It was 1912, and Penney was back in his native land, ready to face LIFE-AS-IT-IS. The bitterness and fear had gone. The loneliness remained.

It was decided to change the name from "Golden Rule Store" to "J. C. Penney Company," since other businesses in the West, to which the name had not the same meaning, were now calling themselves Golden Rule stores.

The time had come for big things, and doing them in a big way. First was the immediate need to establish large credits to cover the cost of expansion.

When Penney went to the banks, he was told that he had reached the extent of his personal borrowings, and if he wanted more credits, then he would have to change his unusual partnership form of business to the customary form of organization. This would mean turning all individual holdings into common and preferred stock, and combining all assets and liabilities.

"But," protested Penney, "that is impossible. What you are proposing would destroy the greatest asset of the J. C. Penney Company—its partnership plan."

The banker agreed. "But you're in business to make money, aren't you?" he asked, reasonably enough. "Isn't that why you want to extend your borrowings, so that you can make more money?"

Once when some Kemmerer residents had called Penney "money-mad," he had done some hard thinking. The time had come for him to do it again. He tried to put in words exactly how he felt about this money-making business. At last he had an answer for the banker.

"I suppose," he said, carefully weighing his words, to be sure he could make his meaning clear, "I suppose if I had a financial mind I would think of money merely as something to be invested in a going concern. I haven't that sort of a mind."

Then, not wishing to seem in the least superior, he hastened to say, "I do not criticize those who have. But, as I now see our business, money is a tool. It is true I started out with the single idea of making money. But now I see our business as an idea that produces money only as a by-product. The direct result produces men to be my partners. Even at the risk of having no bank credits, I will not change that relationship."

If the puzzled banker could not appreciate Penney's firm stand, his partners could. They assured him that he had said exactly the right thing.

But the bald fact remained. To expand, they needed more money. Was there any way around the difficulty? His partners found a way. They joined in what their lawyers called a "subrogation agreement," whereby they entrusted to Penney, as surety for whatever credits he might obtain from the banks, all that they owned in the stores. For most of them, it was all they owned in the world.

Tears stung Penney's eyes when Sams told him what they had done. "They gave me a vote of confidence," he said, years later, "which I prized next to the dying words of my father."

This cleared the way for the incorporation of the J. C. Penney Company under the laws of the State of Utah on January 17, 1913. The homespun partners now found themselves the proud possessors of "classified stock," issued to them in proportion to their store interests, with each store identified on each stock certificate; and with dividends paid against the earnings of each store and distributed according to the individual holdings.

Since the partners were still free to train men, and to open new stores out of earnings, and to share in the earnings of these stores, the partnership idea—the success-spark of the organization—had been preserved. That hurdle had been nicely cleared!

Then came their first annual convention, held in Salt Lake City, and attended by a little group of about twenty-eight Penney men—the humble forerunner of later store conventions so enormous that they had to be divided into regional gatherings meeting in a number of cities.

That first convention lasted a whole week, with the

bewildered partners struggling through what was to them the strange formality and routine of corporate matters. They voted for officers, electing Penney as their president and Sams as their vice president. Attending three meetings a day, they ploughed through a Penney-packed program—the initiation of new managers; store reports; the discussion of individual store plans and problems; shop talk.

Up to now, the new stockholders and associates— Penney would never allow anyone in his employ to be called an employee!—had enjoyed a peaceful, if animated, convention. But, suddenly, the atmosphere changed. Penney was talking about that abhorred topic, CENTRALIZED buying! He saw his audience stiffen, the stubborn set of jaws. But he went right on, presenting his views.

"We must have centralized buying," he insisted. "We must set up a central warehouse, stocked with goods to serve all the stores in the chain—goods bought by an experienced buyer."

He pointed out what a vast improvement this would be on their present system, in which each manager had to take two or more buying trips a year to St. Louis or New York, there to visit the wholesalers and manufacturers, and then, after a long, hard day, meet other Penney men to compare notes and samples, in order to determine the best price for each item, and then decide to place all their orders for each item with the one who offered the best price, all other requirements being equal.

"It wastes time and money to take these trips," said

Penney, "with New York four days distant by fast train. It takes you managers away from your stores where you are needed to train men, and look up new locations."

He had figures and diagrams to show them how much overhead could be saved by being their own wholesalers. Then he looked from one face to another, and read their answer. It was a solid "No!"

And Penney knew the reason why. Years before, he had tried to persuade them to agree to his establishing a big storage warehouse in Salt Lake City, and to employ a specialist to do most of the buying for all the stores. But the managers would have none of it, saying that they preferred to do their own buying. Who knew better than they what their customers wanted? Certainly no stranger sitting in an office away off in some distant city had any idea what a miner, or his wife, in Kemmerer or Cumberland would be likely to shop for. No; leave the buying to the managers who rubbed elbows with their customers and knew their daily needs.

When Penney failed to sell his idea to them, he had gone ahead secretly with his experiment, investing his own money in a big warehouse and hiring an expert buyer to stock it and then operate it. He had then introduced this outsider to his close fellowship of partners, suggesting that they might tell him what lines of drygoods they were interested in so that they could buy from him. But they didn't!

With the big warehouse packed from cellar to attic with merchandise, and only a trickle finding its way to any of the chain stores, Penney had been forced to liquidate his experimental central wholesale business.

Nor was that all. He had then confessed to his managers that although the other fellow's name was on the warehouse, it was Penney's money that had been invested in it, whereupon each manager had taken his quota of the dead, marked-down stock to sell over his own counter. No, sir! Once bitten, twice shy. When the convention week ended, the managers were still refusing to even consider centralized buying.

Penney confided his defeat to a friend of his, a banker.

"Since you feel so strongly that this is the right thing to do," the banker said, "and since you own most of the stock in the company, why don't you compel these partners of yours to go along with you?"

"Compel?" shuddered Penney. "Why, I couldn't possibly do that!"

"Why not?"

"Because they're my partners. We work as one, not as several."

The banker shrugged and smiled. Bankers often found it difficult to understand Penney's financial reasoning.

Long after that first convention, the discussion went on. Once when Penney thought he had them almost persuaded, a partner's question dashed his hopes to the ground.

"I suppose, Mr. Penney," he said, "your plan would

be to locate such a central buying headquarters in Salt Lake City, as you did before?"

"No," replied Penney quietly, "in New York City."

That did it! Those small-town Western boys wanted no part in New York! Some of the senior partners had followed Penney when he moved to Salt Lake City, and were now happily settled there. After serving years in raw settlements and mining camps, they were enjoying the unaccustomed comforts of their new homes. To them, the idea of pulling up stakes and moving to New York was downright preposterous. Why leave familiar ground for the unknown White Way New York?

"To be near our source of supply," pointed out Penney. "New York produces nearly every item we sell. We should have buyers right there to take quick action on manufacturers' overstock; to watch trends. We must train some of our own men to be merchandise buyers."

Our own men! The managers nodded agreement on that. No outsider who hadn't worked his way up the Penney ladder.

"We must train others of our men to be experts in the use of credits and trade discounts. Still others, in a thorough knowledge of shipping routes; of rail and express tariffs, and shipping containers. All these things will be necessary for a chain of one hundred stores."

The thing was getting too big for the small town boys to grasp. Centralized buying . . . experts for this and that . . . New York City!

"We must keep up with our growth," said Penney, his urgent eyes on these partners of his who must be made to see. Finally, they relented enough to agree to his suggestion that he take Sams with him on his next buying trip to New York, and let him, on his return, report directly to them. Sams, they knew, was skeptical too.

Chapter Fifteen

The Expansion Program Begins

Neither Penney nor Sams was ever to forget that particular buying trip. As they called on wholesalers and manufacturers, Penney never lost an opportunity of trying to sell his centralized buying idea to Sams.

"It is the economical, the efficient, the only practical way, Sams. Our customers will benefit in reduced prices by the money we save. Our managers, relieved of the burden of buying as we now do it, will have more time to train their associates. And I, relieved of . . ."

He did not finish his sentence. No need to tell Sams yet, but if this centralized buying once became organized and a going concern, then he, himself, would resign as president and devote his time to Company policies and to the finding of young men for the Penney stores and, having found them, to train them to reach the high standards the job required. He felt that this, at this particular time, was the best thing he could contribute to the rapidly growing business—his liking for young men, his ability to train them, and his deep-down desire to help them to succeed in their chosen work.

As the days rushed by, Penney continued to plead his cause until, finally, Sams agreed to the need for specialists in different branches of store operations, but remained resolutely opposed to setting up centralized buying headquarters in New York.

As the end of the trip grew near, Penney redoubled his efforts. If he could win Sams, he knew the other partners would follow. So, as they retraced and retraced their steps one evening around Madison Square, Penney spoke with desperate earnestness on this matter which was of such immediate importance to him.

All at once he felt his partner's hand on his shoulder. Penney stopped his arguments, halfway through a sentence.

"Are you sure of your judgment?" asked Sams gravely. "Are you still convinced that we ought to move our headquarters to New York?"

"I am sure," replied Penney.

"Then I will come down here," said Sams, and before the relieved Penney could say a word, and with his hand still on his partner's shoulder, Sams went on briskly, "Now, about the men you want to train as experts . . ."

For hours they talked and planned. Sams agreed to help select and train the men, although for the time being he would stay in Salt Lake City.

Their buying trip over, they returned to the waiting partners, who heard Sams' report and loyally accepted the decision.

Penney was elated, but, remembering his first disastrous experiment in centralized buying, he made a simple start. He chose one man from the ranks, and, at his own expense, took this trainee to New York, giving him desk room in his own small office. There they began organizing Penney's knowledge of markets and buying.

No splurge—just a small, careful start. Yet by the following year, it was sufficiently well set up for the Company to take over, with Sams and two assistants coming in to help. Within a few years, that trainee at a desk in a small office, with Penney and a few older partners supplying the know-how, had developed into the New York buying headquarters of the J. C. Penney Company.

Penney had been in business now for only twelve years. He was just past forty, yet his Company had stores in seventy-one towns doing an annual business of $3,560,293.75. It was no longer a provincial enterprise of the pioneer West. Penney now saw his chain as a national one of hundreds of stores. "Beyond two hundred," he dreamed. "Perhaps as many as five hundred. That is not an impossibility."

Did he remember how Berta, in the old Kemmerer days, had once challenged him, "Why not a few stores in the East, too?"

At the end of 1916, Penney, smiling away his partners' objections, resigned from the presidency, although still a young man. He placed in nomination the name of Earl Corder Sams as president, and asked his partners, one by one, to make this unanimous, which they did. Thus Penney was relieved of the administrative and executive detail of the presidency, becoming Chairman of the Board of Directors January 1, 1917.

This step was to open a new way of life to Penney. For one thing, he went back to school! His partners, although somewhat used to his experiments, could make neither head nor tail of this one.

It came about so strangely, all through a book which Penney happened to pick up in the display room of a book concern on the same floor as his office. Penney, no reader, did not even intend to buy a book. He simply had a merchant's interest in knowing how well books sold.

However, the manager of the book display was so courteous that Penney thought he should show his appreciation by buying the book he had chanced to pick up. It was called "Youth and Opportunity," and the author was a man named Thomas Tapper.

Having bought the book, Penney felt he should get his money's worth out of it by reading it. It proved to be one of those little hinges on which big doors swing open. For in the author, Penney saw the specialist he was looking for, to plan a study course for him, and, if at all possible, to tutor him in it.

In the weeks that followed, Penney inquired about this man who wrote so convincingly about Youth and Opportunity. He discovered that he was Dr. Thomas Tapper, then lecturing at several institutions in the Department of Music and Fine Arts and also on the science of personnel and business efficiency. It was a rare combination of talents that intrigued Penney. Through the bookstore proprietor, an arrangement was made for the author and his impressed reader to meet.

Why did Penney, who was making such a sensational success of his life, bother to go back to school? Partly because of that success. Newspapers were asking him for interviews, and church, civic, and trade organizations were inviting him to speak before them, for there was news and inspiration in learning about the principles and practices of a businessman who ran his business by the Golden Rule and became wealthy by doing so.

Penney had been too active, as boy and man, to do much reading. He liked good music, but was at a loss in the world of ideas and literature. He did not express himself as clearly as he wished in public addresses or on paper.

Then, too, he was trying to figure out some way to help the young men in his stores to better educate themselves. Perhaps some course of home study might be worked out for them by this author who was evidently as interested in personnel and business efficiency as he was in music and the fine arts.

Dr. Tapper agreed to tutor Penney, and for eighteen enlightening months, Penney spent half of each business day studying in a quiet little office in Acolian Hall which he had rented in order to be away from interruptions. Here he was given reading assignments on which he was required to give written reports, followed by discussion to test his grasp of what he had read. He grew acquainted with Plato, Ruskin, Thackeray, and other classics, and found this new world fascinating, and wondered why good reading had bored him in his teen-age years at school.

It was an entirely new way of life for Penney, who, for years past, had traveled thousands of miles to visit hundreds of Company stores, sometimes snatching time between trains to inspect one, sometimes spending a whole day behind a counter, teaching a new hand how to sell—and carefully wrap—merchandise.

After his eighteen months of intensive study, Penney took his tutor on a round of store visits. Together, they attended store meetings, and observed that many were not organized and conducted well. While some managers were efficient leaders, others were shy and awkward, muddling through the program as best they could.

"They need help," said Penney, remembering his own young, fumbling years. And Dr. Tapper agreed. But it was not easy for Penney to persuade the learned doctor to give up his profession as music critic and lecturer to head the proposed educational program of a retail drygoods organization. For one thing, Dr. Tapper sincerely doubted that an educational plan of high quality, such as Penney had in mind, could be adapted to such a business. But Penney, with his inherent gift for finding the right key man to help him unlock his problems, continued to urge him, and at last Dr. Tapper agreed to see what he could do. He little knew then how many thousands of young businessmen would be helped to do a better job, and so fill a better position, because of the courses of home study and the books he would write for them.

Penney had a little literary brain child of his own which needed expert care. After resigning as president, Penney had set himself up in a Salt Lake City office as an employment agent for the Company. Here he had advertised for men, and in the first four months had received nearly FIVE THOUSAND APPLICA-TIONS! He had sifted out three hundred for inter-views. Of these, only sixty-three qualified for jobs.

Through this telling experience, he learned how many young people were unemployed simply because they were not trained well enough to get a job, or, if they managed to get one, to hold it. His thoughts then centered on better training for the young men he had recently hired, and for all Penney personnel in the chain of stores.

He had already brought out the first issue of a Company house organ which he called "The Dynamo." This infant brain child of his was an attractive, read-able kit of facts, ideas and suggestions, such as he had been able to deliver in person to the young men in his stores when there were fewer of them. It was a way of keeping in touch with his men and helping them to keep in touch with one another—a shop talk "neigh-boring" in print.

He planned for the little magazine to be a medium for exchange of day-to-day experiences in the store, but as the manuscripts came in to his desk from man-ager contributors, he was keenly disappointed. They were not good enough to serve his purpose.

Now, with Dr. Tapper to guide and develop the new educational plan for any Penney man who cared to avail himself of it—and thousands did!—a "Store Meeting Manual" was prepared to complement "The Dynamo." It gave, among other helpful things, full, clear directions for conducting a store meeting, and the outline of a training topic for each month of the year.

In addition, a new correspondence course for Penney personnel was prepared.

Penney, who believed in partners, soon began thinking of one for busy Dr. Tapper. Although Dr. Short, the Penney family's Salt Lake City pastor, had moved to Spokane, they had always kept in touch. Dr. Short, through the intervening years, had continued to plead, in vain, for Penney to join his church, and Penney, whenever he happened to be in Spokane, had continued to drop in at his old pastor's home to enjoy one of Mrs. Short's famous dinners of stewed chicken and dumplings.

The more Penney thought of it, the more he was convinced that Dr. Short and Dr. Tapper would make a wonderful team. So he invited his old pastor to come and help them with the Company's educational department.

It was an inspired choice. Dr. Short, a gifted speaker, was ready to travel all over the country, to fill speaking engagements in store towns, or wherever people were interested in hearing how the Golden Rule had—and could—work in business. Proving, one rewarding year after another, what miracles can be wrought by one book, if it falls into the right hands!

Chapter Sixteen

The Golden Rule Plan
Reaches a Zenith

The next ten years saw much growth, and some changes of policy in the J. C. Penney Company. Sams' first impression of the early stores—with their merchandise hanging from the ceilings, their homemade counters, and makeshift desks of oilcloth - covered boxes—was that they were "junky." Now that he was president, he began to place bigger stores in better locations. Much more money was needed for expansion.

Penney and he went to New York bankers to get further credit. Three years previously when the partners had gone to New York to establish their first line of credit, a banker, after what seemed like endless questions and reflective delays, had lifted puzzled eyes from the Company's incorporation papers, and said, "This is a pretty wild and wooly proposition, but maybe we can help you." Which the bank had done, to the extent of $75,000.

But now there were twice as many stores—and partners!—and much more was needed. The bankers insisted that Penney and Sams would have to change the incorporation papers of their business to conform to the usual corporation practice, under which the Company would own and control all the shares in its own name.

It was the same old struggle, with Penney fighting to keep the partnership plan intact, and the bankers refusing to extend further credit unless the incorporation papers were changed.

"We can't do it," protested Penney, his determined gray eyes meeting the cold steel of the bankers'. "The strength of our Company is in the partnership arrangement that distributes stock in ratio to earnings."

The bankers' only reply was to recommend that Penney consult a certain legal firm in New York.

Trust such an important matter to strangers! Not he, declared Penney.

The choice of lawyers was entirely up to him, the bankers told him, but he had no choice in the matter of changing the Company's articles of incorporation.

"That is," they said, "if you expect to establish any further credit with this bank."

Something had to be done. That year, while vacationing, Penney had met a brisk young New York lawyer who had made valiant efforts to teach him to play a good game of golf. He had not succeeded, but Penney had liked him. He decided to seek out this young man,

Ralph W. Gwinn, and ask him to study this knotty problem, and make recommendations.

Gwinn did this, presenting his bill. The amount of it scandalized the thrifty Penney. Four hundred dollars for a few paragraphs of legal suggestions! Outrageous! He immediately dismissed young Gwinn, and sought another firm of New York lawyers—and fared much worse! For this firm charged him two thousand, five hundred dollars for advice of about the same number of words.

This was little short of highway robbery to Penney. He called Gwinn back, thus beginning what was to be years of close association with him, as the Company's attorney, and later, as Penney's staunch friend and business partner.

Gwinn had done a good job. The bankers were satisfied, and so was Penney, for, in spite of the necessary changes, the precious partnership plan remained intact.

While all this was being threshed out, the store managers were studying new styles in women's wear. Both Penney and Sams could remember when about all they needed in ladies' apparel to stock their stores was a full line of kimonos and wrappers. But those simple days were gone forever. Now the Company had buying facilities in St. Louis and St. Paul, as well as New York, and Penney customers were being assured in display advertising, "You can now have garments that are just as stylish as those of the well-dressed women who parade along Fifth Avenue and Broadway, for you are not more than six days removed from New York style and fashion."

Since most of the Penney stores were still in small towns, this was headline news for the Main Street housewives.

This was the time, too, when all Penney managers were becoming community - conscious, taking their place as leaders in local affairs. Both Penney and Sams had been born and raised in small towns where one had neighbors. They wanted their managers to be neighborly, and urged them to take part in all worthwhile activities in the towns where their stores were located. Once started, this became a regular part of Company policy, existing to this day.

Penney stores kept up with the times, but one thing never changed. This was their Penney "code," known in Kemmerer days by a high-sounding name, but now called simply, "Penney Principles," and by that name, with wording unchanged, it has come down to the present time.

These principles are:

1. To serve the public, as nearly as we can, to its complete satisfaction.

2. To offer the best possible dollars' worth of quality and value.

3. To strive constantly for a high level of intelligent and helpful service.

4. To charge a fair profit for what we offer—and not all the traffic will bear.

5. To apply this test to everything we do, "Does it square with what is right and just?"

In 1919, there were 197 stores, and in the summer

of that year Penney married again. His bride was Mary Kimball, a highly-educated woman, with unusual musical talent, and with a character of great beauty. She lived but a few years after the marriage. Then the mother of his son, Kimball, passed on.

Penney filled the void with work, and more work. With new stores springing up in all directions, he traveled here, there, and everywhere. Then came the doctor's warning to slow down, and get out in the sunshine and fresh air—and rest. A physical examination for a new life insurance policy confirmed the doctor's advice.

Sunshine suggested Florida; fresh air, a farm. Rest? Penney had never learned how. He bought a winter place for his family on the East coast at Belle Isle in Biscay Bay, a stone's throw from the mainland.

And he turned farmer again, returning to the soil for brief snatches of Nature's restoration. He bought a small estate in Westchester, at White Plains, New York. It consisted of a home and sixty-five acres. To this he joyfully added horses, cattle, sheep, Berkshire hogs, poultry. It was good to be back on the farm again.

He had learned a great deal about farmers and their problems while on his constant business trips. Most of the stores were in rural sections, and their success often rested on the prosperity of the farmers. As Penney well knew, one of the farmer's greatest needs was for better cattle. What could he do about that?

A wonderful way presented itself when, in 1922, he was able to purchase the 720-acre Emmadine Farm in Dutchess County, New York. Here he established the foundation of "a practical, workaday institution for the improvement of purebred Guernsey cattle, and the dispensation of tested scientific information to the farmers of the country."

As he inspected his selected Guernseys, with the best brood cows money could buy, and four herd sires, among them the famous Foremost 39191, did he remember his one family cow in Kemmerer, and how he had said to young Earl Sams, "While I am away, as my first man, your job is not only to run the store, but to milk the cow. You can milk, can't you?"

The Penney chain of stores was fast nearing its 500th link, when news came that Mr. Hale of the J. M. Hale and Brother drygoods store in Hamilton, Missouri, wished to sell his store, and retire.

Hale's! Here, twenty-eight years earlier, the ailing Reverend James C. Penney had brought his son, Jim, seeking employment for him. Here, Mr. Hale had given the thrilled Jim his first steady job. Here, Jim had suffered the jibes of the older clerks—"Look at Mose! He's earning all of $2.27 a month! He's gonna be a rich man some day!"—and here, on one memorable day, he had found himself.

Now he had a chance to own that store. He hurried to Hamilton, warmly greeted his old boss, and purchased the store, as the residents stood around, marveling, "Can you beat it?" Then he enlarged and renovated it, and waited, so that by way of special celebration, he could open it as the 500th store in the J. C. Penney Company.

Also, in the twenties, Penney bought his father's

old farm outside Hamilton, Missouri, renaming it, "The Home Place," and, in later years, he added to this six other farm tracts, all within a few miles of it. He felt his father would like that.

Meanwhile, away off in Florida, the very air reeked of speculative money, for the real estate boom was making men millionaires overnight. Zooming in 1924, it reached its peak in the first half of 1925, and collapsed in September, 1926.

Penney, by now an immensely wealthy man, was too cautious to be drawn into the whirlpool, but he did start looking for timber land to buy as an investment.

He found a tract of 120,000 acres in Clay County on the west bank of St. John's River. Twenty thousand acres had already been cleared. There was a 100-mile network of roads, twenty-five miles of which were paved to a width of sixteen feet. There were 300 houses, 125 of them being good substantial farm houses.

He acquired the whole tract in the name of the Penney-Gwinn Corporation, which was in no way connected with the J. C. Penney Company.

Here was the chance for another experiment! Why not divide a large part of the tract into small Penney farms, and sell them to farmers from all over the United States on a partnership basis? Just as there had been drygoods salesmen who never could have owned their own stores but for his manager-partnership plan, so there must be many good, hardworking farm men who would never be able to own their own farms unless they had help—not only financial, but agricultural information and guidance.

He named his newly - purchased acres Penney Farms, placed 3000 range cattle on the land, established an experimental poultry plant of 4000 birds, provided for a dairy herd, and a drove of swine. An Institute of Applied Agriculture was set up, so that the settler-farmers could be trained in the best scientific practices of agriculture, under a staff of experts.

Then, as Penney had once given careful thought to the selection of new store personnel, he now made plans for finding the right type of farmer to settle at Penney Farms, and live in one of the sturdy farmhouses, and work his twenty-acre plot, with the goal of ownership to lighten his labors.

Penney made it clear from the start that the settler-farmer must be a regular church-goer, and must abstain from strong drink, and not smoke cigarettes. There were now 745 J. C. Penney Company stores, and he asked the managers of these to help select the farmer prospects, seeing to it that they measured up to the Penney standards of character and industry.

Soon the settlers began to move in; first forty, then fifty more, and the Penney partnership-farm experiment was underway.

Chapter Seventeen

A Program of Philanthropy Begins

Penney's old pastor, Dr. Short, spoke often of the moral responsibility of men of means to give generously to those good causes the support of which depended largely on contributions from private individuals. Penney agreed with him, and for years had been considering setting up a J. C. Penney Foundation for such a purpose.

He thought of the people whose needs had touched him deeply in the past. He remembered those nights when, heartsick and hopeless, he had wandered through the wretched streets of the Bowery, and had seen the human derelicts huddled in the doorways. He remembered the little mission there, and its hymn of hope.

He remembered the sickly children of the city streets who had played in the filth of the alleys.

He remembered his minister - father's financial struggle, and his own youthful longing to find a way in which he could happily make a living.

One day his Foundation would help maintain a Bowery Mission; a vacation home in the country for city waifs; and a community of homes for aged ministers and their wives. But this he did not know.

He knew only one thing, positively. He wanted his Foundation to help young people solve some of the problems of youth.

He had been mulling over this for some time, looking for a key person to help him put it into effect. In 1922, at a dinner of the Committee of 1000 in New York, he met him! Among the guests was a handsome, well-built young man, reserved and dignified, who spoke eloquently and forcefully of his belief in young people. For years he had worked with thousands of them. He knew their worth.

Penney learned that this enthusiastic champion of youth was Dr. Daniel A. Poling, then pastor of the Marble Collegiate Church at Fifth Avenue and 29th Street, New York City; and that he was also leader of the International Christian Endeavor Society.

Penney knew that here was his man! He arranged for his partner, Ralph Gwinn, to meet him, and later, in 1925, he told Dr. Poling of his decision to set up a J. C. Penney Foundation, and asked him to consider being its director.

At that time Dr. Poling was absorbed in his weekly radio program which he called Conference for Young People. It took the form of an inspirational address, followed by a period of questions and answers pertaining to the problems of youth.

Penney assured Dr. Poling that this program would

be helped by his Foundation, and Dr. Poling agreed to come in with Penney on a part-time basis.

There followed a radio youth guidance program that swept the nation. At first, broadcast over one local station, it was soon being heard over thirty-eight. While Dr. Poling spoke every Sunday afternoon in one of the public rooms of the old Waldorf-Astoria to an audience of youngsters packed in like sardines, thousands of others were listening in their own living rooms or in churches to his powerful, youth-slanted sermons.

Letters by the thousands began pouring in from young people—at least half of them seeking educational or vocational guidance. To further help them, the J. C. Penney Foundation set up a vocational department, equipping it with a library and a secretarial staff, and with a research division to cooperate with the National Youth Radio Conference.

Exciting things were happening in Penney's business world, too. Now he was getting additional stores not singly, but in bunches!

It had pleased him to be able to buy the store that had given him his first start. Now he was to have the chance to buy the chain of stores owned by Callahan and Johnson, the two men who had made it possible for him to own his first store in Kemmerer.

In 1926, T. M. Callahan came to Penney, saying, "I'm tired. Will your Company buy my twelve stores?" Two years later, Guy Johnson came with a similar request. He had twenty stores he wanted to sell. Penney and Company bought all thirty-two. At the end of 1926, there were 747 stores in the chain and, for the first time in its history, the Company had sales in excess of $100,000,000!

Penney, the business magnate, was happy over this, but Penney, the philanthropist, was heeding a Voice. It had spoken to him in the dark watches of one night, bringing him a wonderful plan for Penney Farms. "It was as clear as though a voice had spoken," he told Ralph Gwinn next morning.

The plan was to build at Penney Farms a community of Florida homes for aged ministers and their wives, as a permanent memorial to his parents.

In June, 1926, ground was broken for this memorial to be built in the heart of Penney Farms, and the cornerstone was laid for the Penney Memorial Chapel, which was to be its soul.

Less than a year later, the dream was a glorious reality. There stood a group of beautiful homes of Norman-Gothic design, clustered around a little church, an architectural gem that looked as if it had been lifted bodily from some Old World village, carried overseas and placed in that peaceful spot, bringing with it all the prayers and benedictions of bygone generations.

Each house was built to shelter several couples, each in its own apartment consisting of three rooms and a bath, and fully furnished and equipped for housekeeping. The exterior of the homes were finished in beige; the roofs, a soft red.

Inside the little church was a new and beautiful organ, installed by Ralph Gwinn in memory of his own sainted mother, and a screen of carved, illuminated wood that Mr. Penney's two sons had given in memory of their mother who had passed on.

The dedication of this dream Memorial Home Community was one of the most moving moments of Penney's life. Attending the week-end dedicating ceremonies were many notables—writers, travelers, statesmen, doctors of divinity, and college presidents. Dr. Short was there to deliver the dedicatory sermon. The services were marked by brilliant oratory and colorful ceremonies, but for most of the assembled guests the memory they carried home in their hearts was of the afternoon service, during which sixteen different members of the Community "family" spoke their thanks for their new home.

Sixteen old men, veterans of long years of service for their Lord, representing sixteen different denominations. Margaret E. Sangster, who attended this dedication, described them in these words:

"Men who had preached in tiny hamlets; men who had spoken God's Holy Word in city houses of prayer; men who had been missionaries, and men who had been circuit riders. All working for the love of a blessed Saviour, and for the salvation of the lost sheep, rather than for financial recompense. They have come along the years, striving, working, hoping, loving! Perhaps at times wondering about the roof over their heads and the food for the next meal. But never fearing. Never doubting."

During the morning exercises of the Sunday of dedication, at which Dr. Poling presided, Penney sat in the shadow of the pulpit, visibly moved as the buildings were given to the service of God. Once someone saw his lips move for just a second, as if silently saying a word. Was he whispering, "Pa"?

When it came time for him to present the Memorial Home Community for aged religious workers and their wives, to the J. C. Penney Foundation, he said in a voice that shook a little with emotion in spite of himself:

"I feel myself but the humble instrument in the hands of God to carry on the work for which my parents gave their lives. What I have done, and all that I have done, is little enough when I think of what they did. Such measure of success as I may have achieved, and all that I am under God, I owe to those parents, to the depth of their faith, the unfaltering character of their influence and training, and to the unfailing example they held ever before my eyes.

"Beyond all other investments that I have made, this investment has yielded me already a return in satisfaction that I have found nowhere else. And so today, with a mind full of sacred memories—memories that remain although the ones calling them forth have passed from this life into the better and larger life beyond—and with a heart moved to thoughts that my lips cannot express, I give these buildings to the J. C. Penney Foundation, for the purpose heretofore agreed upon, as a memorial to the Reverend James Cash Penney, my father, and his beloved wife, Mary Frances Penney, my mother, and as a home for men and women who have followed the Christ whom my parents served, pouring out their lives for the holy cause in which my parents lived and died."

Between the time of the ground-breaking for the Memorial Home Community and the dedication, a great joy had come into Penney's life. He had gone abroad, and in Paris had married young, attractive Caroline Autenreith, the present Mrs. Penney.

Of this marriage, Penney says, "It has been blessed in more ways than I can enumerate. The influence of this woman has brought about the full measure of happiness that is mine today."

He goes on to confess, "Before our first child was born I fear I was a little too hopeful that it would be a boy. I just couldn't picture myself as the father of a daughter. I wanted only sons, but my wife presented me with a daughter."

He adored her at first sight. "I shall never forget," he says, "I shall never be able to explain the transformation that came over me as I stood looking for the first time at this tiny girl-baby, who was soon to grow up and become another of the women who have influenced my life. For influence it she has! And for much good—this daughter, and also her sister who came along a few years later."

It was this wife and these daughters who taught Penney—who still didn't know enough to quit working!—the meaning of such strange words to him as relaxation and recreation. In these happy years, he little knew how near were the agonizing days when he would need his wife's strength and sweetness of soul to help him survive them.

By now the business had grown so large that Penney knew the time had come to abandon the old arrangement of selling partnerships in individual stores, and to revise the corporate setup of the Company accordingly.

In the year 1927 the old plan gave way to the new. Store managers and New York office executives went on salary, plus other compensations based on profits.

Golden Rule Penney saw to it that managers' money-making opportunities would not be lessened because individuals could no longer be permitted to open their own stores. He and Sams worked out a profit-sharing plan whereby a manager shared in the profits, and in most cases the manager's share exceeded his salary.

In one case, for instance, a young manager and his wife were struggling along on a salary of $135 a month. He had been transferred to this larger store, and quite expected that his salary would be increased to $150. But since it wasn't, the disappointed couple made the best of it, and practiced Spartan economy.

When his first year was up, he received a letter from the treasurer at headquarters. It contained his "compensation, guaranteed by contract" for a share in the net profits of the store he had managed. The check was for approximately eleven thousand dollars!

Chapter Eighteen

A Lifetime of Toil Swept Away

Now came the years when larger chains of stores were absorbed by the J. C. Penney Company, and there were offers of mergers from the country's largest mail-order houses.

The first was from J. B. Byers, with his chain of 116 stores extending across the Western and Far Western states. He wished to dispose of his stores, but, in doing so, he wanted to be sure that his employees would not suffer because of the sale.

"I like the way you treat your people," he wrote to Penney, "and I feel that with you they would be in good hands."

It was a happy day for him when, as he announced the merger to his managers, he could tell them, "You can rest assured that all good managers will be retained in their present stores, under managerial contract on the same basis as the J. C. Penney managers."

While the negotiations were underway for the absorption of the Byers' stores, there came a letter from

F. S. Jones who had a chain of 54 stores he was anxious to sell. These were located mostly in the Northwest. In May, 1927, these were absorbed into the J. C. Penney Company, with all their 54 managers, "highly pleased with the merger."

Thus, in two years, 170 stores were added to the J. C. Penney chain.

The Company was doing a gross business of over one hundred and seventy-six million dollars when Montgomery Ward & Company, the Chicago mail-order firm which was then planning to expand into the retail field, came to the J. C. Penney Company, suggesting the possibility of a merger.

Penney's board of directors thought the suggestion should be given careful consideration, and a committee was appointed to meet with Montgomery Ward's president to discuss the matter. But finally the answer was a polite "No."

Sams wrote to the president of Montgomery Ward & Company, "The board of directors of our company, all of whom are active in business, feel themselves in a peculiar position of trust with regard to the preservation of the J. C. Penney Company's plan of work and compensation. Knowing the situation as they do, they would be unwilling to take stock in a combination that might endanger the continuation of such a plan. . . ." There followed a sentence showing his hope that such big businessmen would understand this Golden Rule decision: "I trust that this statement of the case will not seem altogether too sentimental to you."

Another Chicago mail-order concern was expanding into the retail field, and soon a letter came from the president of Sears, Roebuck & Company suggesting a merger.

For a time it looked as if this might go through. Julius Rosenwald, chairman of Sears, had a great admiration for the Penney organization and its methods; and R. E. Woods, then president of Sears, had already in mind a tentative plan of operation, should the merger be made. Roughly, it was this:

The operating functions of the merged companies were to be divided into three—a mail-order division; stores in large cities; and stores in smaller cities and towns. The mail-order division was to continue under Sears' trained executives; the stores in small towns and cities were to be placed directly under Penney-trained merchants; the personnel in the large city stores must be absorbed.

In regard to the merchandise, all textiles and shoe buying—Penney's specialties—were to be in charge of a merchandise manager who would be a Penney man. All heavy lines, or lines not carried by Penney, were to be in charge of a manager who would be a Sears' man.

Weeks of intensive investigations followed. A group of executives from Sears worked with an equal number of Penney's executives as a committee "to explore every possibility." The men from Sears went into and through every operation of the Penney organization—buying, management, testing, personnel training, etc. They took merchandise from Penney stores to test in their own laboratories. Then men from Penney's went through the same procedure with the Sears, Roebuck operations.

Much hung in the balance. At long last, Penney's representatives turned in their reports to the top executives of the Penney Company. They recommended the merger.

Now there were more important meetings, this time of the senior executives of the two companies, with their lawyers and accountants. Then discussions lasting several weeks. All seemed to be moving along to where the two big companies would be merged into one enormous organization.

But both Penney and Sams were deeply concerned about the effect the merger might have on their young executives, fearing it might lessen their opportunities for advancement.

So a letter was sent to the president of Sears, much like the one that had been sent to Montgomery Ward, expressing the Penney management's conviction that "it could not deliver to a new company the values we now enjoy," and that by merging, "the savings to the public would be negligible and our younger executives would have lesser rather than greater opportunities." That was the end of the plan to merge.

Penney was pleased that his young men could now climb steadily to the top, but he was keenly aware of what he would now face in tough competition as the two mail-order concerns went ahead with their plans to open hundreds of new retail stores in the small towns where his own stores were located.

He knew, too, of the dark clouds of disaster that

were gathering on the business horizon—the threat of the depression. A merger might have been an easy way out, since not only Penney but all the top men in the organization could have sold out for large sums of money. But they stayed in, to face whatever came.

After the collapse of the real estate boom in Miami, Penney had refused to believe that the city's future was dead and buried. To prove his faith in a better day, and help it to come, he invested millions in the City National Bank of Miami, Fla. His reputation as a multi-millionaire who had built his fortune from scratch, drew other investors to the bank. From a substantial stockholder, he rose to be chairman of the board.

Meanwhile, the philanthropies in which he was interested were feeling the hard times. They desperately needed his financial help. He poured vast sums into his Foundation, borrowing for this from five banks, using his personal holding of shares in the J. C. Penney Company for collateral.

Then came the national calamity, the black depression that lasted month in, month out, year in, year out —the panic of 1929 to 1932, when financial ruin drove many a big business magnate to suicide.

But Penney was not afraid. He felt he was safe. He was confident that nothing — not even so terrible a thing as this nation-wide depression — could touch a man as wealthy as he.

He borrowed more millions to meet the needs of "Christian Herald," Memorial Home Community, Penney Farms, National Youth Radio Conference, Emmadine Farm, and Foremost Dairy Products. All were feeling the leanness and distress of the times.

So was the City National Bank of Miami. As the depression deepened, and the general financial situation became even blacker, Penney pledged his personal holdings to borrow large amounts of cash to keep the bank sound. He put in a cash total of over a million and a half dollars, which he lost. The Penney-Gwinn Corporation loaned the bank $2,334,000, which it lost.

In spite of all that could be done to save it, the City National Bank was forced to close its doors the day before Christmas, 1930. And now Penney was to go through his Gethsemane, as shocked and suffering, he was to hear his personal character and moral responsibility attacked.

"Never before, to my knowledge," said Golden Rule Penney, "had the honor of any dealings of mine been questioned. It was a cherished reputation. Now, in a matter of hours, I was confronted by conditions and accusations which I could never have imagined."

In October, 1929, common stock in the J. C. Penney Company had been listed on the New York Stock Exchange for the first time in its history. Until then it had been a closed corporation. A few days later, the market crashed. After that, the Penney Company shares plunged from $120 to $13. In 1932, Penney's 360,000 shares in the J. C. Penney Company had to be sold to satisfy his creditors, and his fortune of forty million dollars was practically wiped out.

Penney was now a poor man. What crushed him most was that he could no longer support his many philanthropies. He gave "Christian Herald" to Dr. Poling, "with no strings attached," closed the agricultural project at Penney Farms, and retrenched in every way. Dr. Poling was able to secure new financing and now in his later years Mr. Penney has conducted one of the Journal's most popular features, "Lines of a Layman."

He was 56 years old, and flat broke. His world in ruins, he returned to Whitehaven, and to his wife, Caroline, whom he had so happily married only a few years ago. They sent the children to stay with their grandmother in Phoenix, Arizona, dismissed the servants and outside men, closed the house except for two rooms, and lived in these as best they could, with Mrs. Penney doing the housework and Penney doing the outside chores.

Penney clung to one thing through shattering blow on blow. It was just a scrap of paper on which he had written a Scripture verse from Psalm 91. "He shall cover thee with His feathers, and under His wings shalt thou trust. His truth shall be thy shield and buckler."

The power of money was no longer his. Now he was to learn more about the power of God.

Chapter Nineteen

God's Plan for Penney

Penney had seen the fruits of a lifetime of toil swept away in a few brief months. From being a man whose very name spelled success, he was now a pitiful failure —just another beaten man with no apparent future, and too old to start over.

Not knowing what else to do, he tried the therapy of manual labor. Before the crash, his employed men had been at work at Whitehaven preparing a new section of pasture land. But after he had been forced to let them go the land had returned to wilderness.

Penney, now near physical and nervous breakdown, began to take on where ten men had left off. He cut brush, pulled weeds, cleared off stones, every muscle aching. He tried to forget the attacks on his character—the sword-stab that he had "run out on the bank"; the painful pricks of the false rumor that he was still rich, since he received a dollar a day from every store in the Penney chain; that he had been christened plain James Penney, and had added that middle "Cash" just to advertise his cash-and-carry business.

He tried to remember how his father had once said, "Jim, don't harbor bitterness. People see things as they see them. It takes time."

He flinched as he recalled that his father also had said, "Jim will make it." He had made it—and lost it. Why? What had brought him to such a pass that, in late middle age, he could not even support his wife and children?

He was still Chairman of the Board of the J. C. Penney Company and as such was committed to an itinerary of speaking engagements. He was soon due to speak at a noon luncheon in Battle Creek, Michigan. He dreaded the ordeal. Miserably, he thought, "What kind of a message can I, a business failure, bring them now?"

Yet he braced himself to go. A promise was a promise. Somehow, he labored through the speech, conscious of two things—that he had not done very well, and that here at the luncheon was an old friend of his, Dr. Elmer Eggleston with whom he had gone to school in Hamilton.

By this time he was feeling so ill that he decided to ask his friend, who was a staff doctor at the Kellogg Sanatorium, to examine him. The doctor discovered that Penney's whole right side was broken out with an aggravated case of shingles. He promptly ordered the suffering man to bed, assigning day and night nurses to the case, and prescribing strong sedatives to give him a chance to sleep and rest.

As soon as the effect of the sedatives wore off, Penney had a new worry to torture him. Where was the money coming from to pay for all this hospital care? He began to beg the doctor to let him get along without the night nurse.

At last the doctor agreed. And that night Penney knew positively that before morning came, he would die! He took the sedative at nine, but was wide awake by ten. He got out of bed and wrote his farewell letters to his wife and children and to a few close friends. It seemed to him that he could actually see his spiritual self standing outside his weary body just waiting for him to breathe his last.

His letters finished, the envelopes addressed and sealed, he went back to bed to await his end. Instead, he fell asleep, awaking at a very early hour, surprised, but not pleased, to find himself still alive. It was not yet time for the day nurse to come on duty so there was no one to stop him when he put on his clothes and shuffled downstairs.

He was not at all sure why he was up and around when all other patients were still asleep. Vaguely he thought of breakfast—he had always been an early riser—but the dining room was not yet opened.

There he was, all alone in the grey pre-dawn silence. Before him stretched unknown areas of solitude . . . emptiness . . . aloneness. In his sick mind, he was sure that his friends—even his dear wife and children —considered him a failure and no longer had any feeling for him but pity. A desolate sense of his own helplessness bore down on him like a heavy cross. What was to become of him?

"And, suddenly there was an angel . . ." Just as

before, when bitter and bereft, he had walked the Bowery streets, the ministering angel came in the form of a well-known hymn. Winging softly along the silent corridor, he heard distant voices singing:

> "Be not dismayed, whate'er betide
> God will take care of you . . ."

With faltering steps, he sought the sound and found it came from the mezzanine where people had gathered to start the day with God.

> "No matter what may be the test,
> God will take care of you;
> Lean, weary one, upon His breast,
> God will take care of you . . ."

He went in and slumped down in one of the back seats. "Whate'er betide." With the words, a whisper of hope came to the sick man. Now someone was softly reading a Scripture passage. He leaned forward to hear:

"Come unto me, all ye that labour and are heavy laden, and I will give you rest." The passage was followed by a brief prayer.

Penney was praying, too—such an agonized prayer as he had never prayed before. "Lord," he groaned within himself, "of myself I can do nothing. Will You take care of me?"

Penney, fluent lecturer on a thousand occasions, has never been able to put into words just what happened to him then. He only knows that it was a miracle; that God sent an instant answer to his broken, humble cry for help.

In one of his books he tries to describe it. He writes, "I had a feeling of being lifted out of an immensity of dark space into a spaciousness of warm and brilliant sunshine. . . . A weight lifted from my spirit. I came out of the room a different man, renewed. I had gone in bowed with a paralysis of spirit, utterly adrift. I came forth with a soaring sense of release, from a bondage of gathering death to a pulse of hopeful living. I had glimpsed God."

Penney went back to his room a changed man. Knowing the road ahead was going to be one of hardships and heartbreak, he now had the will to fight his way back. Gone was self-pity, blame of others for what had befallen him. In their place was severe self-analysis and self-criticism. He had found a new humility.

Worried Sams had been in daily communication with the hospital, inquiring about his partner's progress. The date of a convention was fast approaching, and Penney was on the program. Would he be able to make it?

Until now, the doctor's report had been discouraging, but since Penney's spiritual experience, so remarkable a change for the better had taken place that the doctors agreed to let him go to the first meeting of the convention, which was in Louisville. The first; no more!

"God will take care of me," Penney told himself, rejoicing as he felt strength given him to take part in the program. He went on from there to the next engagement, and then to the next. He could still make speeches that informed, encouraged, and inspired others. That was something he had not lost.

Two months after that morning when he had prayed, "Lord, will You take care of me?" he was back home, spending Christmas with his family.

Penney had always been self-sufficient, never one to rely on anyone. Until he had been brought low by adversity, he had always enjoyed a quiet assurance of his own adequacy. Now he began to lean on God; to try to find God's plan for his life, and for the use of his talents and experience. He had always read the Bible, taking one with him on all his business trips. Now he began to study it.

Black, bitter days lay ahead—nerve-rasping trials when accusers tried to prove deliberate wrong-doing on his part as contributing to the bank failure. He had desperate need to touch that scrap of paper in his pocket.

There were other things, too, to add to his humiliation. One was being compelled to go back on the J. C. Penney payroll. In the seven years he had worked at Kemmerer, he had received a salary. But since 1909, it had been his proud boast that he had not accepted a cent in salary from the Company, his sole income being derived from earnings of his shares in the business stores.

It was necessary for him to receive this salary for only three years, but he confesses, "It called, in a special way, for all the humility I could summon."

Gradually, he got on his feet again. A younger brother and two friends loaned him money, not knowing—not really caring—if it could ever be paid back. Two of the banks from which he had borrowed to help his good causes had not called his loans, and this helped.

He was still in great demand as a public speaker, and in the late thirties he was asked to address a normal school assembly, taking as his subject, "The Application of Christian Principles in Business." He was instantly drawn to his audience of young student-teachers, and told them of the six principles he, himself, had adopted for his own life's program. They were simple, but they made for a worthwhile life. They were:

"I believe in preparation. I believe in hard work. I believe in honesty. I believe in reposing confidence in men. I believe in appealing to the spirit in men. I believe in the practical application of the Golden Rule, as taught by the Master two thousand years ago, 'Therefore all things whatsoever ye would that men should do to you, do ye even so to them, for this is the law and the prophets!' "

After the meeting, a young local minister came up to him with the eager request, "Mr. Penney, will you repeat this talk in my pulpit this Sunday morning?"

"Oh, no," exclaimed Penney, "I couldn't do that. I've never spoken from the pulpit. I'm only a businessman."

But the young preacher persisted. "There is a lot of meat in that talk," he enthused, "and I want my people to hear it."

Penney still hesitated. "I'd feel out of place," he demurred. But the minister was persuasive—and young —and Penney at last consented to occupy the pulpit the following Sunday morning.

He was staying at his father's old farm, Home Place, Hamilton, Missouri, at the time and it was pleasant to drive through the bright spring sunshine the twenty-seven miles to the Chillicothe Christian Church.

A veteran speaker, he had no qualms until after the minister had escorted him to the chancel. Then he noticed something that filled him with sudden panic. The Lord's Table was spread for a Communion service!

In spite of all Dr. Short's pleading, Penney had never joined a church. He had never attended a Communion service; did not even know its appointed order. He leaned over to whisper nervously to the minister, "I'm afraid this is rather embarrassing. As this is to be a Communion service, I must tell you that I have never partaken."

The young minister did not look as aghast as Penney had expected. He whispered back, "You're a Christian, aren't you?"

The nervous Penney nodded. He hoped he was that.

"Well, then," whispered the young minister, "there's no reason why you can't partake at the Lord's table." After which he busied himself arranging the markers in hymn book and Bible, and, before he knew it Penney was joining the congregation in singing the first hymn, "The King of Love My Shepherd is." He was still nervous when they reached the lines:

Thou spread'st a table in my sight,
Thy unction grace bestoweth;

It was then that he heard the Voice again—could it be his minister-father's?—saying, "Be not afraid."

His old pastor could never understand why Penney had never joined a church. Neither could Penney. Was it because when, as a boy of ten, carried away by a revival service, he had wanted to join the Baptist church in Hamilton, Missouri, and he had been discouraged by his father's quiet, "Are you sure you are ready, son?"

Was it the bitter memory of the cruel way that little church had excommunicated his father? Or was it the memory of his deeply-religious mother's whispered prayer as she went about her home duties, "Lord, be merciful to me, a sinner!" If anyone so good as she considered herself a sinner, how black must he be in the eyes of the Lord! Far too evil to join any church.

Was it because he feared people might say he had joined the church for business reasons? Or was it simply because some of the church members he knew were such downright hypocrites?

The service was nearing its climax. They were about to partake of the Lord's Supper. He was still undecided. "Fear not," the Voice had said. Should he heed it—or not?

He heeded it, and for the first time in his life partook of Communion.

That night he wrote to his wife, "I have come to the point where I want to be baptized and join the church."

Chapter Twenty

The Miracle of Mr. Penney

All through the depression years, the Penney chain of stores went on steadily growing. Those lean years, when, in order to stay in business at all, one had to exert every possible effort, made Penney men even better managers. Those lean years also brought customers who in better times had shopped elsewhere, to a Penney store where they could make every nickel count.

The chain grew, but the stores took in less money. The year following the market collapse the Company, for the first time in its history, failed to show a gain in sales. It dropped again in 1931, and in 1932—a total difference of over fifty-four million dollars since 1929.

But in spite of this the Company kept expanding its operations, opening new stores in 78 cities in the first three years of the depression.

In 1937 there were 1,523 Penney stores; in 1940, 1,586. Nor did this persistent growth cease through all the political restrictions of the anxious years preceding

World War II, and government war-time controls. Through all the problems of acute shortages in merchandise and personnel, the Company kept moving ahead to a sales volume of over five hundred and forty-nine million dollars in 1945.

Not being classified as an essential industry, the Company lost many of its key personnel to the armed services. Their places were filled by women, who did a remarkable job.

Said Penney, "I want to tell you that it was the women who really kept our stores going throughout the war years. We had over 5,000 men in the service —and women did men's jobs, and did them well."

During those gallant years, Sams wrote, "Hundreds of our stores do not have a single Penney man besides the manager. Women are writing orders, trimming windows, making show cards, keeping the stores clean, selling most of the merchandise, doing every job in the store. Penney women have kept the Company in business."

That was a tough, strength-draining stretch, covering the depression and the war years, and Sams, now past retirement age, asked to be relieved of the responsibilities of the presidency. He had served as president for almost thirty years.

He gave a rousing address to the assembled Penney personnel at his last conference.

"This Company has just begun to scratch the surface of its possibilities! There is no such thing as reaching—or even approaching—the top of the ladder of accomplishment and achievement. The best way to do anything has not yet been found. There are greater things ahead!"

A few years later he died, and in 1950, Penney dedicated his second book, "Fifty Years With the Golden Rule," to him in these words:

"To Earl Corder Sams, my friend and associate from Kemmerer days, this book is dedicated with respect and gratitude for a life which was a sure sign of that New Life in Christ, which endures."

Sams' usual farewell at the close of a friendly conversation or a convention speech, had been a cheery, "Go on with the good work!"

The good work did go on. A. W. Hughes, who once had been summer tutor of Penney's small sons and nephews, and, as a zealous manager of his first store had been reproved for making too much money, was now president of the Company, having climbed up the ladder of promotion, cautiously step on step.

Penney, now honorary chairman of the board of directors, was slowly, but surely, rebuilding his financial fortune. But the making of money no longer held an important place in his thinking. Instead, he was deeply concerned with spiritual values, not "treasures upon earth."

Since his experience at Battle Creek, life had taken on an entirely new meaning for him. He felt himself to be a spiritually new man as if, on that night when he was sure he was going to die, the old, broken, bitter failure he thought himself to be, actually did die, and a new self had arisen as if in a glorious resurrection.

Through this miracle he felt that God had not only brought him back to life, but, in doing so, had a purpose for him to fulfill. He prayed long and earnestly to be shown what that purpose was, and to find a way whereby he could use his talents and experience to the glory of God.

He had been baptized by Dr. Poling at a private service in Philadelphia. He had also joined the church, being received into the Memorial Church at Penney Farms, not only because it was a memorial to his parents but also because it was nondenominational. The good people who made up this "household of faith" had come from all points of the country. They were missionaries, YMCA and other Christian workers, men and women of deep evangelical faith. It was a church home into which he wanted to be received.

Then, through his acquaintance with the Reverend Sam Shoemaker, rector of Calvary Protestant Episcopal Church at Gramercy Park, New York, he was led to join an informal activity of the parish—a businessmen's prayer meeting. About twenty men met at the close of business every Monday for a short session of prayer and exchange of experiences.

Penney found an inspiring fellowship with this group of businessmen. He learned that all of them had obstacles to overcome, and, realizing that their help lay in a closer walk with God, were seeking it through prayer.

Another to give him a spiritual helping hand was his good friend, Ralph W. Gwinn—the man Penney had once dismissed for charging him what he consid-

ered too high a bill for services rendered. Gwinn was
keenly interested in the "Laymen's Movement for a
Christian World," and invited Penney to meet some of
the leaders in it. He liked their simple pledge of only
twenty-five words: "As a Christian layman, I will try
to find my part, and exert my strength, into building
Christianity into the everyday life of the world."

Soon Penney was asked to speak at a Laymen's
Movement Conference in Bronxville, his topic to be,
"The Application of Christian Principles in Business."
He had first-hand knowledge of his subject, and spoke
with inspiring conviction.

After the meeting he was approached by Dr. James
Fifield, pastor of the First Congregational Church of
Los Angeles, at that time the largest church on the
West Coast.

"Mr. Penney," he said, "that is a message which
you ought to go out and give all across the country."

Penney's immediate reaction was exactly the same
as it had been when the persuasive young Missouri
minister had invited him to occupy his pulpit.

"Oh, no," he refused, backing away from the very
idea, "I couldn't possibly do that!"

It was then that Dr. Fifield said the very thing that
was needed to embark Penney on this nation-wide program of speeches.

"Yes, you can," he said positively, "if you will only
give yourself now as wholeheartedly as you have given
your money in the past."

Giving himself! That was the answer to Penney's

prayer to be shown the way! It was the beginning of his speaking tours around the country, and in Canada, for the Laymen's Movement. Sometimes he spoke before large urban groups, sometimes in little rural houses of prayer no bigger than the Log Creek Church in Missouri where his father had once preached. God was now in full charge of his life. Said Penney, happily at peace, "God wanted to possess me, not merely my possessions."

In the years that followed, the J. C. Penney Company stores grew to 1,600, 1,650, 1,700! The founder of this enormous chain served as president until 1917, as chairman of the board from then until 1959, and is still a member of the board of directors of the Company. Now in his 88th year, he is still as active as ever in day-to-day Company affairs. When in New York, he comes daily to his office in the huge building which houses the executive and buying offices of the J. C. Penney Company. He rises at 6:30 a.m., arrives at his office at 8:30, and leaves at 5:30 p.m.

His day buzzes with activity. He employs a number of secretaries to answer voluminous correspondence with active and retired managers and other associates.

In the summer, he commutes from Green Farms, Connecticut, where he owns a home on about four acres of land.

When not in his office he is touring the country, attending store openings or visiting other stores where he delights in doing some selling himself.

In April, 1962, he revisited his home town and the store which he had purchased from his first employer,

Mr. Hale. Recalls a salesman, "Most of his three days' stay in town were spent at the Hale-Penney store wrapping packages, selling Easter clothing, and just having a grand old time."

He celebrated his 87th birthday on September 16, 1962, in typical Penney style. He combined the celebration with a whirlwind trip to the Eastern States exposition, a luncheon with several governors, and a visit to store No. 1405.

The store visit began Saturday morning when he met all the associates, walked through the different departments, and answered on-the-spot questions from a local reporter. After time out for lunch, and a quick trip to the Fair Grounds of the Exposition to register as a New York State representative, he was back at the store. This time he greeted customers, answered more questions for a radio interview, and shared with all comers the great birthday cake provided by Manager Joe Shively.

On Sunday he attended the luncheon for all Northeastern governors at the invitation of John A. Volpe, Governor of Massachusetts, and later spent the afternoon on the fair grounds.

He enjoyed a quiet family party with some old friends on Monday night. The next day he was on the go again. He visited an exhibition of Angus cattle during the day, then returned in the evening to the Springfield store to greet about 75 home economics teachers who were there to meet him so that they could learn more about the Company's program for education—a program that includes film strips, teachers' publications, and workshops.

On Wednesday he headed for his summer home in Connecticut, having finished one of the most strenuous celebrations in anyone's timetable.

In the slick, interest-packed edition of the "Penney News" — imposing descendant of the humble little "Dynamo"—that gave the account of Penney's 87th birthday celebration, was headline news of further growth of the Company—the story of a new office being opened in London, England, for European operations; of Penney buyers in Japan, Hong Kong, Thailand; of the launching of a new Catalog of Sales experiment in seven Midwestern states in the U. S. A. The good work is going on!

Many honors have come to this man who built that shacky little Kemmerer store with its crate and deal box fittings into a chain now operating in 49 states and which in 1961 grossed one billion, five hundred million dollars.

He is the holder of honorary degrees in no less than fifteen colleges and universities.

In 1953, he was elected to the Hall of Fame in Distribution at the Boston Conference on Distribution. He also was elected to the Oklahoma Hall of Fame in 1955. In 1953, he received the Horatio Alger Award of The American Schools and Colleges Association; the Tobe Award for Distinguished Contribution to American Retailing, and the Award for Outstanding Christian Service presented by The Church Federation of Greater Chicago.

Twice he has received the Freedoms Foundation at

Valley Forge Award for bringing about a better understanding of the American way of life.

He is a director of Allied Youth, organized to educate young people to the evils of alcohol; vice-president of the Laymen's Movement for a Christian World, a leading member of Rotary, and a 33rd Degree Mason.

He owns a 4,000-acre Missouri farm, dedicated to the improvement of cattle and crops, and is a substantial stock holder in Foremost Dairies, which he helped to start about thirty years ago.

He is the author of four books and many pamphlets and magazine articles. He has also collaborated in the writing of two other books. There have been numerous articles written about his life and business. He travels thousands of miles a year on Company business, and speaks before civic, trade, religious, and youth groups, as well as participating in radio and TV programs.

And with it all, he still has the friendliness of a small town neighbor. He has dignity and distinction and Old World manners—but he is proud to tell you that he buys all his clothes in a Penney store with the exception of detached collars which he has especially made for him.

He has alert gray eyes, so young that he needs glasses only for reading, snowy white hair, and a neatly-trimmed moustache. His walk is brisk and his carriage erect.

He wears a bright bow tie—the J. C. Penney trademark—and carries in one pocket his father's old jackknife. In his lapel he wears a service button, as do the Penney managers. On it are the letters HCSC, standing for the motto of his Company—Honor, Confidence, Service, Cooperation.

"What I have done," he insists, "anyone could have done. I haven't any special attainments."

This is Golden Rule Penney.